David L. Pollard

A Student's Vocabulary of Biblical Hebrew

Listed *ate*

D BY

des

York

CHARLES SCRIBNER'S SONS
NEW YORK

13151719 **M/P** 2018161412

PRINTED IN THE UNITED STATES OF AMERICA
SBN 684-41323-X
Library of Congress Catalog Card Number 61-7224

Contents

Foreword

A major exercise for the student of any foreign language—and one that persists long after he has mastered the chief difficulties of such phenomena as script, pronunciation, grammar, and idiom—is the acquisition of a good working vocabulary. For the English student of Biblical Hebrew, the task is further complicated by the significant paucity of etymological relationships between the vocables of Hebrew and those in his own language. Moreover, not only does Hebrew writing look vastly different, but also when its words are pronounced, their sounds rarely suggest meanings in English identical with their actual definitions.

For many years, students of Biblical Hebrew who have sought a tool to facilitate their learning of vocabulary have become familiar with William R. Harper's *Hebrew Vocabularies*, first published in a private edition in 1882, and then brought out in a fifth enlarged edition by Charles Scribners' Sons in 1893. Despite its usefulness, this fifth edition was never reprinted, though a greatly abridged form of it appeared as an appendix in all editions of Harper's *Introductory Hebrew Method and Manual*, most recently (1958) brought out in a paperback edition by the University of Chicago Press. In 1956, J. Barton Payne, Professor of Old Testament at Trinity Seminary in Chicago, published his own *Hebrew Vocabularies* (copyright by Baker Book House), based upon three lists drawn from the 1893 edition of Harper's original work, to which Prof. Payne made certain additions and corrections, completely reworking the list of Hebrew Particles (Part III in his arrangement). This was followed in 1959 by John D. W. Watts' *Lists of Words Occurring Frequently in the Hebrew Bible* (copyright by E. J. Brill, Leiden, Netherlands, but distributed in America by the Wm. B. Eerdmans Publishing Co.), which utilized the same three lists of Harper selected by Payne (though somewhat further abridged), but arranged them in a more useful format, and helpfully provided stem indications, where appropriate, for the verbs. Dr. Watts also made revisions and corrections in comparison with the Köhler-Baumgartner Hebrew-Aramaic Dictionary (*Lexicon in Veteris Testamenti Libros*, Leiden, 1953).

Now both of these recent efforts to simplify, shorten, and correct Harper's *Hebrew Vocabularies* have been a welcome auxiliary to students of Biblical Hebrew, but in the present writer's opinion, their full effectiveness has been hampered by rigidly adhering to Harper's main organizational principle, viz., listing the words alphabetically in groups of descending frequency categories (500-5,000, 300-500, 200-300, etc.), with verbs, nouns, and particles separated into three distinct lists. From a methodological and pedagogical standpoint, such an arrangement leaves something to be desired, especially when its basic intent to ease the student's burden of memorizing large numbers of Hebrew words is carefully considered. Hence the *raison d'être* for this new effort to reformulate the vocabulary lists of Biblical Hebrew.

A fundamental truism of learning theory is that we increase our knowledge by association, particularly by relating things which, by their nature, belong together. Many languages, including Hebrew, form a large number of their words from basic verbal ideas. Thus a great many of the non-verbal parts of speech—nouns, adjectives, adverbs, even prepositions and other particles—trace their derivation from verbal roots. When a student sets about to learn Hebrew verbs, he should therefore do so in conjunction with their nominal and other cognates. For when he studies a verb and its cognate(s) listed together, he often becomes aware of natural mnemonic devices which help him to remember the words so arranged. Moreover, not only is he then able to see more clearly the relationships between these words, but he is also encouraged to learn a larger number of them than would be the case were the verbs divorced from their derivatives in separate lists. As a pedagogical aid for learning vocabulary, the listing of verbs with their cognates is not new; it has been regularly followed by those who prepare printed vocabulary cards for students of various ancient and modern languages. For New Testament Greek, it has been successfully done by Bruce M. Metzger in his useful *Lexical Aids for Students of New Testament Greek* (privately printed in an enlarged edition, 1955). Even William R. Harper in section VIII of his *Hebrew Vocabularies* (1893 edition) made use of it for Biblical Hebrew, but unfortunately this section was never reprinted in subsequent editions and revisions of his work, and never has it been worked out with the comprehensiveness that this present apparatus attempts.

In the following pages the Vocabularies are

arranged in three major lists. Throughout the first two, words are grouped according to frequency *and* their cognate relationships. List I is the largest, containing every verbal root and its respective derivatives (if extant) that occur in the Hebrew Bible from about ten to over five hundred times. The English definitions have been placed in columns next to the Hebrew with sufficient space to permit the student conveniently to study and review the Hebrew without having to look directly at the English. The list is subdivided into frequency categories, much in the fashion of Harper's work. Frequency ranges are employed for all words occurring 70 or more times in the Old Testament, while words which occur less than 70 times are listed with their exact number of occurrences (all figures are based on word counts made from Solomon Mandelkern's *Veteris Testamenti Concordantiae Hebraicae atque Chaldaicae*, reprinted 1955). Verbs with an incidence of 70 or more are listed alphabetically, but those below 70 are catalogued in a descending frequency order, most often determined by the frequency of their derivatives. That is, verbs having cognates occurring more than 500 times are listed first in each of the frequency categories below 70, while verbs with cognates belonging in the 24-10 range are listed last. Obviously, this arrangement could not be pursued in detail, since a number of verbs have several cognates which vary in frequency ranges. In general, however, the position of a verb in the groups below 70 is determined by its cognate with the highest frequency figure(s). With the cognates also, only frequency ranges are specified for those appearing 70 or more times, but precise enumerations are indicated for those below 70. If a verbal root has more than one cognate, the derivatives are listed in decreasing frequency order.

List II contains every verbal root in the Old Testament with a frequency of less than ten, but which also has a cognate or cognates with a frequency of more than ten. The format of this list much resembles that of List I. Verbs are not listed alphabetically, but in accordance with the frequency of their derivatives. Exact frequencies are recorded for those derivatives occurring less than 70 times. When specific Biblical texts are cited in parentheses after the English definition of the verbal root, they denote the only occurrences of the root in the Hebrew Bible.

List III contains the common nouns and other parts of speech which occur in the Old Testament ten or more times, but which have no extant verbal cognates in the Hebrew Bible. The words are arranged alphabetically in the frequency categories above 70, in descending order in accordance with their exact frequency occurrences below 70.

Most of the English definitions are based on those given (in German) in the Köhler-Baumgartner dictionary. Only basic definitions are given.

An Appendix listing most of the Hebrew proper and place names of the Old Testament with an incidence of 70 or more is added for the convenience of beginning Hebrew students, who sometimes have difficulty with this type of word. The names are arranged in decreasing frequency order. Where such derive simply from a single verbal root, they may be found listed with that root in the appropriate vocabulary division.

Since none of the lists are consistently alphabetical in their arrangement, an Index has been provided to facilitate the rapid finding of the Hebrew words. This will be especially useful for those who merely wish to look up the cognate(s) of a certain root, or to see whether a specific word has an extant cognate or not, or to check the frequency of a particular word. Obviously the apparatus should never be used as a surrogate for the lexicon.

In learning words, the student should select from all three lists as he proceeds through the vocabularies, rather than taking each as it comes. A suggested order of learning is as follows:

1. List I A., II, nos. 1-8, III A.
2. List I B., II, nos. 9-23, III B-C.
3. List I C., II, nos. 24-38 III D.
4. List I D., II, nos. 39-47, III E.
5. List I E., II, nos. 48-63, III F.
6. List I F., II, nos. 64-101, III G.
7. List I G., II, nos. 102-192, III H.

Though the accuracy of the apparatus has been carefully checked by the author and others, a work of this kind is highly susceptible to errors and omissions, and those who use it will probably find some of both. The author will always appreciate being informed of any corrections or additions that should be made. Though I take full responsibility for all inaccuracies, I wish to express my gratitude to all those who have been helpful, in one way or another, in the preparation of the vocabularies for publication. I especially owe a debt of thanks to Prof. Prescott H. Williams, Jr., who carefully examined the preliminary mimeographed copy of the manuscript, on the basis of which he made many corrections and suggestions; to Prof. David Noel Freedman, who graciously offered the use of his own vocabulary list containing exact frequency counts, and who studied the next-to-final draft of the present work; to my students at Union Theological Seminary, particularly Mr. James Wood, who spent many hours meticulously checking most of the frequencies and making corrections where necessary, but also many others, who, as beginning students in Hebrew, have used these lists in learning Hebrew vocabulary, and as a result of their efforts, have suggested several ways of improving the original manuscript. Finally, I am grateful to my colleagues in the Old Testament Department, Profs. James A. Muilenburg and Samuel L. Terrien, for their interest and encouragement in this project.

GEORGE M. LANDES

SIGLA AND ABBREVIATIONS

1. *Sigla*

(1)	A number in parentheses preceding (reading from right to left) a root, cognate, or other word, designates a particular set of definitions or meanings, among others, attached to the same sequence of consonants elsewhere in the Hebrew Bible. The numbering follows that given in the Köhler-Baumgartner lexicon.
(1)†	The above symbol followed by a dagger indicates that another word having the same consonants does *not* occur in this apparatus.
*	An asterisk placed before a Hebrew word indicates that the word is nowhere extant in its absolute form in the Hebrew Bible.
(?)	A question-mark in parentheses following the listing of a Hebrew cognate indicates that its derivation from the root under which it is placed is uncertain.
>	Indicates derivation from a root or other word.
<	Indicates a word goes back to a specified root.
(13, Ex.)	If only the name of an Old Testament book is indicated after a frequency figure, it means that the word occurs in that book alone.
(Hi.)	When a verb has a meaning or set of meanings which are regularly (though not necessarily exclusively) expressed in one or more particular stems, these stems are noted in parentheses after the appropriate English definition(s).
(Qal)	If a verb is extant only in the Qal conjugation, the word Qal in parentheses occurs before the Hebrew rendering of the root.
(#)	For words marked with this symbol see page 44.

2. *Abbreviations*

adv.	adverb	Is.	Isaiah
Am.	Amos	Jo.	Joel
c.	common	Josh.	Joshua
Cant.	Canticles	Ju.	Judges
cf.	compare	juss.	jussive
Chr.	Chronicles	Kgs.	Kings
conj.	conjunction	Lam.	Lamentations
cstr.	construct	Lev.	Leviticus
Da.	Daniel	m.	masculine
den.	denominative	Mic.	Micah
Deut.	Deuteronomy	Neh.	Nehemiah
dim.	diminutive	Ni.	Niphal
Ec.	Ecclesiastes	Num.	Numbers
Es.	Esther	p.	page
Ex.	Exodus	Pi.	Piel
Ez.	Ezra	plu.	plural
Ezek.	Ezekiel	Pu.	Pual
f.	feminine	prep.	preposition
Gen.	Genesis	Prov.	Proverbs
Hab.	Habakkuk	Ps.	Psalm(s)
Hi.	Hiphil	ptc.	participle
Hith.	Hithpael	s.	singular
Ho.	Hophal	Sa.	Samuel
imp.	imperative	suff.	suffix
int.	interjection	t.	times
Jer.	Jeremiah	vs.	verse

בְּנִי לִדְבָרַי הַקְשִׁיבָה . . .
אַל־יַלִּיזוּ מֵעֵינֶיךָ שָׁמְרֵם בְּתוֹךְ לְבָבֶךָ׃
Prov. 4 : 20–21

LIST I

Verbal Roots,

Their Nominal and Other Cognates,

Occurring Ten or More Times

An Alphabetical Listing of Addenda to LIST I

אָבֵל (2)[1] water-course, brook (13)
[Insert as No. 117a., p. 19.]

אֵמֶר (1)† word (49, 21 in Prov.)
[Insert as No. 2a., p. 3.]

דרךְ to tread, bend the bow (62)
דֶּרֶךְ a. way, road, journey; custom (over 500)
[Insert between Nos. 17c. and 18, p. 10.]

המם (Qal) to discomfit, disturb (14)
[Insert between Nos. 169a. and 170, p. 20.]

זנח (2)† to reject (21)
[Insert between Nos. 86 and 87, p. 18.]

חַיִּים life, lifetime (100-199)
[Insert as No. 10b., p. 4.]

חפז to hurry away (in alarm, fright) (10)
[Insert between Nos. 222 and 223, p. 21.]

יָהּ Yah (shortened form of יהוה) (25, 19 in Ps.)
[Insert as No. 5b., p. 3.]

יקץ[2] (Qal) to awake (10)
[Insert between Nos. 223 and 224, p. 21.]

לון to murmur against (Ni., Hi.) (19)
[Insert between Nos. 109 and 110, p. 19.]

לֵוִי Levi (200-500)
[Insert as No. 174a., p. 20.]

לָכֵן therefore (100-199)
[Add to No. 16a., p. 4.]

[1] For אֵבֶל (1), see p. 13, no. 84a.

[2] Cf. with I G. 82, p. 18.

מִקְנָה purchase (15)
[Insert as No. 31b., p. 9]

מַשְׂכִּיל Hi. ptc. used as title for a type of poetic composition in Ps. (14)
[Insert as No. 36b., p. 9.]

נוד to be aimless; homeless; shake (the head (25)
[Insert between Nos. 162 and 163, p. 15.]

סוךְ to anoint with oil (10)
[Insert between Nos. 226 and 227, p. 21.]

עַל־כֵּן therefore
[Add to No. 17a., p. 3.]

צֶמַח growth, a sprout (10)
[Insert as No. 119a., p. 14.]

קָדֵשׁ, קְדֵשָׁה (1)† sacred person, temple prostitute (10)
[Insert as No. 45d., p. 7.]

קַל, קַלָּה light, swift, fleet (13)
[Insert as No. 30b., p. 9.]

רַגְלִי one who walks on foot (12)
[Insert as No. 6b., p. 11.]

רוה to drink one's fill (15)
[Insert between Nos. 163 and 164, p. 20.]

שׁור (1)† (Qal) to behold, regard (16)
[Insert between Nos. 149 and 150, p. 19.]

שׁחח to bow down (17)
[Insert between Nos. 138a. and 139, p. 19.]

שׁעה to gaze, look at (14)
[Insert between Nos. 182 and 183, p. 20.]

תְּשׁוּעָה deliverance, salvation (34)
[Insert as No. 15c., p. 4.]

I A. Verbs Occurring Over 500 Times

אכל	**1**	to eat, devour; to feed (Hi.)
אֹכֶל	a.	food (45)
מַאֲכָל	b.	food (30)
אָכְלָה	c.	food (18, 10 in Ezek.)
אמר	**2**	to say
אִמְרָה	a.	saying (35, 18 in Ps. 119)
בוא	**3**	to go in, enter, come; to bring in (Hi.)
תְּבוּאָה	a.	increase (41)
מָבוֹא	b.	entrance (25)
דבר (2)[1]	**4**	to speak (Pi.)
דָּבָר	a.	word, thing (over 500)
דְּבִיר (#)	b.	back room of temple (16, 11 in I Kgs.)
היה	**5**	to be, happen
יהוה	a.	Yahweh (over 500)
הלך	**6**	to go, walk
ידע	**7**	to know
דַּעַת	a.	knowledge (70-99, 40 in Prov.)
מַדּוּעַ	b.	wherefore? why? (70-99)
יִדְּעֹנִי	c.	familiar spirit, sooth-sayer (11)
ילד	**8**	to bring forth, bear
יֶלֶד	a.	male child, boy (70-99)
יַלְדָּה (f.)		girl
תּוֹלְדוֹת*	b.	generations (39)
מוֹלֶדֶת	c.	kindred (21)
יָלִיד*	d.	son, slave born in the household (13)
יצא	**9**	to go forth, out
צֹאן	a.	flock (200-299)
מוֹצָא	b.	issue, exit, utterance (27)
תּוֹצָאוֹת	c.	sources, extremities, outlets (23, 14 in Josh.)
צֶאֱצָאִים	d.	offspring (11)
ישב	**10**	to sit, dwell, inhabit
מוֹשָׁב	a.	seat, dwelling (44)
תּוֹשָׁב	b.	sojourner (14)

[1] For דבר (1), see p. 26, no. 21

לקח	**11**	to take
לֶקַח	a.	teaching, understanding (9, 6 in Prov.)
מות	**12**	to die
מָוֶת	a.	death (100-199)
נכה	**13**	to smite (Hi.)
מַכָּה	a.	smiting, blow (45)
נשׂא	**14**	to lift up, bear, carry
נָשִׂיא	a.	prince (100-199)
מַשָּׂא (1, 2)	b.	burden, tribute; oracle (67)
מַשְׂאֵת	c.	a lifting up, gift (16)
שְׂאֵת	d.	dignity (14)
נתן	**15**	to give
מַתָּן, מַתָּנָה (f.)	a.	gift (22)
נְתִין*	b.	(only plu.) those given to the temple, temple-servants (17, all in the Chronicler)
עבר (1)[1]	**16**	to pass over, transgress
עֵבֶר	a.	side, region; (prep.) beyond (70-99)
בַּעֲבוּר	b.	(prep.) on account of; (conj.) in order to (49)
עִבְרִי	c.	an Hebrew (32)
עלה	**17**	to go up
עַל (2)†	a.	(prep.) upon, against, over (Over 500)
עֹלָה	b.	burnt-offering (200-299)
מַעַל (2)[2]	c.	upwards, above (100-199)
עֶלְיוֹן	d.	the upper, highest (53)
מַעֲלָה	e.	ascent, step, stair (46, in first vs. of Ps. 120-134)
עֲלִיָּה	f.	upper room (20)
מַעֲלֶה	g.	ascent, rise; stand, platform (19)
עָלֶה	h.	leaf, leafage (17)
תְּעָלָה (1)† (?)	i.	water-course, conduit (9)
עמד	**18**	to stand
עַמּוּד	a.	pillar, column (100-199)

[1] For עבר (2), see p. 28, no. 77
[2] For מַעַל (1), see p. 14, no. 106a

עִמָּד*	b.	(prep., only with suff.) with (45)
עשׂה	**19**	to do, make
מַעֲשֶׂה	a.	work (200-299)
צוה	**20**	to command (Pi.)
מִצְוָה	a.	commandment (100-199)
קוּם	**21**	to rise, stand
מָקוֹם	a.	place (300-500)
קוֹמָה	b.	height (46)
קָמָה	c.	standing grain (10)
קרא (1)[1]	**22**	to call, meet
מִקְרָא	a.	convocation (25, 12 in Lev.)

[1] For קרא (2), see p. 12, no. 19

ראה	**23**	to see; to appear (Ni.); to show (Hi.)
מַרְאֶה	a.	sight (100-199)
רֹאֶה	b.	seer (12)
מַרְאָה	c.	vision, mirror (12)
שׂים (Qal)	**24**	to set, place
שׁוּב	**25**	to turn, return
מְשׁוּבָה	a.	backsliding, apostasy (12, 9 in Jer.)
שׁלח	**26**	to stretch out, let go, send
שׁמע	**27**	to hear, obey
שְׁמוּעָה	a.	report (27)
שֵׁמַע	b.	report (17)

I B. Verbs Occurring 200-500 Times

אהב	**1**	to love, like
אַהֲבָה	a.	love (40)
(אֹיֵב) איב	**2**	to be hostile towards (all but once in Qal ptc.: enemy)
אסף	**3**	to gather
בנה	**4**	to build
בֵּן	a.	son (over 500)
בַּת (1)[1]	b.	daughter (over 500)
תַּבְנִית	c.	likeness, pattern (20)
בקשׁ	**5**	to seek (Pi.)
ברך (2)[2]	**6**	to bless
בְּרָכָה	a.	blessing (68)
זכר	**7**	to remember
זִכָּרוֹן	a.	memorial (24)
זֵכֶר	b.	remembrance (23)
חזק	**8**	to be strong; to seize, grasp (Hi.)
חָזָק	a.	firm, strong (56)
חטא	**9**	to miss (a mark), sin
חַטָּאת	a.	sin, sin-offering, expiation (200-299)
חֵטְא	b.	sin (35)
חַטָּא*	c.	sinner; sinful (19)

[1] For בַּת (2). see p. 41, no. 117

For ברך (1), see p. 29. no. 98

חיה	**10**	to live
חַי ; חַיָּה (f.)	a.	living, life (300-500); beast, wild animal (100-199)
יסף	**11**	to add
יוֹסֵף	a.	Joseph (200-299)
ירא	**12**	to fear
יָרֵא	a.	afraid of, fearful (61)
יִרְאָה	b.	fear, reverence, awe (45)
מוֹרָא	c.	terror (12)
ירד	**13**	to go down
ירשׁ	**14**	to subdue, possess, dispossess
תִּירוֹשׁ	a.	new wine (38)
רֶשֶׁת	b.	net (22)
יְרֻשָּׁה	c.	possession (14)
ישׁע	**15**	to save, deliver (Hi., Ni.)
יְשׁוּעָה	a.	deliverance, salvation (70-99)
יֵשַׁע	b.	help, salvation (36, 20 in Ps.)
כון	**16**	to be firm, established (Ni.); to set up, establish (Polel); to prepare, make ready (Hi.)
כֵּן (1, 2)	a.	thus so; firm, upright (over 500)
מְכוֹנָה	b.	base (24, 15 in I Kgs. 7)
מָכוֹן	c.	foundation, place (17)
כלה	**17**	to cease, come to an end, finish, complete
כָּלָה	a.	complete destruction (22)

Hebrew	No.	Meaning
כרת	**18**	to cut off, fell, exterminate; make a covenant (with בְּרִית)
כתב	**19**	to write
כְּתָב	a.	writing (17, 9 in Es.)
מלא	**20**	to be full; to fill, fulfill (Pi.)
מָלֵא, (f.) מְ	a.	full (63)
מְלֹא	b.	fullness (38)
מִלֻּאִים	c.	consecration, setting (15)
† (1) מלך	**21**	to reign, be king
מֶלֶךְ	a.	king (over 500);
מַלְכָּה		queen (35, 25 in Es.)
מַמְלָכָה	b.	kingdom (100-199)
מַלְכוּת	c.	kingdom (70-99)
מְלוּכָה	d.	kingdom (24)
מצא	**22**	to find
נגד	**23**	to make known, report, tell (Hi.)
נֶגֶד	a.	(prep.) before (100-199)
נָגִיד	b.	leader (44)
נטה	**24**	to turn, stretch out
מַטֶּה	a.	rod, staff, tribe (200-299)
מִטָּה	b.	bed, couch (29)
מַטָּה	c.	beneath (18)
נפל	**25**	to fall
נצל	**26**	to deliver (Ni., Hi.)
סור	**27**	to turn aside; to take away, remove (Hi.)
עבד	**28**	to serve
עֶבֶד	a.	servant (over 500)
עֲבוֹדָה	b.	service (100-199)
ענה (1) [1]	**29**	to answer
פקד	**30**	to visit, number, appoint, miss, take care of, muster
פְּקֻדָּה	a.	oversight visitation, punishment (32)
פִּקּוּדִים*	b.	precepts (24)
פָּקִיד	c.	overseer, officer (13)
† (1) רבה	**31**	to be numerous, be great; to multiply, make many (Hi.)
אַרְבֶּה (?)	a.	locust (23)
שכב	**32**	to lie down
מִשְׁכָּב	a.	bed, place or act of lying (46)
שמר	**33**	to keep watch, guard
שֹׁמְרוֹן	a.	Samaria (100-199)
מִשְׁמֶרֶת	b.	guard, obligation, service (70-99)
מִשְׁמָר	c.	guard, guardpost, group of attendants (20)
שפט	**34**	to judge; to enter into controversy, plead (Ni.)
מִשְׁפָּט	a.	judgment, custom (300-500)
שְׁפָטִים	b.	acts of judgment (16, 10 in Ezek.)
שתה	**35**	to drink
מִשְׁתֶּה	a.	banquet (45, 23 in Es.)

I C. Verbs Occurring 100-199 Times

Hebrew	No.	Meaning
אבד	**1**	to perish; to destroy (Pi.); to exterminate (Hi.)
אמן	**2**	to be steady, firm, trustworthy, faithful (Ni.); to believe (Hi.)
אֱמֶת	a.	trustworthiness, stability, faithfulness, truth (100-199)
אֱמוּנָה	b.	faithfulness (49)
אָמֵן	c.	(it is) sure, certain; amen (25)
בוש	**3**	to be ashamed
בֹּשֶׁת	a.	shame (30)
בחר	**4**	to choose
בָּחוּר	a.	young man (44)
בָּחִיר*	b.	chosen (13)
מִבְחָר*	c.	choice (12)
בטח	**5**	to trust
בֶּטַח	a.	security, trust (42)
מִבְטָח	b.	trust (15)
בין	**6**	to understand
בַּיִן*	a.	interval;
בֵּין		(cstr.) between (over 500)
תְּבוּנָה	b.	understanding (42)
בִּינָה	c.	understanding (37)

[1] For ענה (2), see p. 9, no. 26;
ענה (3), p. 25, no. 13;
ענה (4), p. 20, no. 190

בכה	**7**	to weep
בְּכִי	a.	weeping (30)
גאל (1) [1]	**8**	to redeem
גְּאֻלָּה	a.	redemption (15, 9 in Lev.)
גדל	**9**	to become strong, great; to bring up, let grow, nourish (Pi.)
גָּדוֹל	a.	great (over 500)
מִגְדָּל	b.	tower (51)
גֹּדֶל	c.	greatness (13)
גְּדוּלָּה	d.	greatness (12)
גור (1) [2]	**10**	to sojourn
גֵּר	a.	stranger (70-99, 43 in Num.-Deut.)
מְגוּרִים*	b.	dwelling-place, sojourning-place (12)
גלה	**11**	to reveal, uncover; depart, go into exile
גּוֹלָה	a.	captivity (42)
גָּלוּת	b.	exile(s) (15)
דרשׁ	**12**	to seek, inquire
מִדְרָשׁ	a.	exposition (2, II Chr. 13:22, 24:27)
הלל (2) †	**13**	to praise (Pi.); to boast oneself (Hith.) (87 t. in Ps.)
תְּהִלָּה	a.	praise (56, 29 in Ps.)
הרג	**14**	to kill
זבח	**15**	to slaughter
מִזְבֵּחַ	a.	altar (300-500)
זֶבַח	b.	sacrifice (100-199)
חוה	**16**	to bow down (Hishtaphel)
חלל (1) [3]	**17**	to be defiled (Ni.); to pollute, profane (Pi.); to begin (Hi.)
תְּחִלָּה	a.	beginning (23)
חָלִילָה	b.	(int.) far be it from . . . (preventive negative exclamation) (20)
חנה (1) † (Qal)	**18**	to encamp
מַחֲנֶה	a.	camp (200-299)
חשׁב	**19**	to account, regard, value
מַחֲשֶׁבֶת	a.	thought (54)
טמא	**20**	to be unclean
טָמֵא, טְמֵאָה (f)	a.	unclean (70-99, 46 in Lev.)
טֻמְאָה	b.	uncleanness (37, 18 in Lev.)
ידה (2) †	**21**	to thank, praise, confess (Hi., Hith.)
תּוֹדָה	a.	song of thanksgiving (32)
הוֹד	b.	splendor, majesty (24)
יטב	**22**	to be good
יכל (Qal)	**23**	to be able
יתר	**24**	to be left, remain (Ni., Hi.)
יֶתֶר	a.	remainder (100-199)
יֹתֶרֶת	b.	caul (of liver) (11, 9 in Lev., 2 in Ex.)
יִתְרוֹן	c.	profit; pre-eminence (10, Ec.)
כבד	**25**	to be heavy, honored
כָּבוֹד	a.	honor, glory (200-299)
כָּבֵד (1)	b.	heavy (40)
כָּבֵד (2)	c.	liver (14, 9 in Lev.)
כסה	**26**	to cover, conceal (Pi.)
מִכְסֶה	a.	covering (16)
כפר	**27**	to cover; expiate (Pi.)
כְּפִיר	a.	young lion (31)
כַּפֹּרֶת	b.	cover, lid (26, 19 in Ex.)
כֹּפֶר (4) †	c.	ransom, reparation (13)
לבשׁ	**28**	to put on, clothe
לְבוּשׁ	a.	clothing (32)
לחם (1)	**29**	to fight (Ni.)
מִלְחָמָה	a.	war, battle (300-500)
לֶחֶם	b.	bread (200-299);
>לחם (2)		(den.) to feed a person (6)
לכד	**30**	to seize, capture
נבא (den.)	**31**	to prophesy (Ni., Hith.)
נָבִיא	a.	prophet (300-500)
נוח (1) †	**32**	to rest, settle down, make quiet; lay, deposit (Hi.)
נִיחוֹחַ	a.	sweetness, odor (43, 36 in Lev.-Num.)
מְנוּחָה	b.	rest, quietness (21)
נגע	**33**	to touch, reach, come to
נֶגַע	a.	stroke, plague (70-99, 60 in Lev.)
נגשׁ	**34**	to draw near, approach
נוס	**35**	to flee
נחם	**36**	to be sorry, repent (Ni.); to comfort, console (Pi.)
נסע	**37**	to depart

[1] For גאל (2), see p. 20, no. 195

[2] For גור (3), see p. 21, no. 196

[3] For חלל (2), see p. 27, no. 41

מַסַּע	a.	journey or journeying, stage (12, 7 in Num.)
סבב	**38**	to turn, surround
סָבִיב	a.	(prep.) round about, surrounding (300-500)
ספר (den. of סֵפֶר)	**39**	to write, count, number; to recount, report, enumerate (Pi.)
סֵפֶר	a.	book (100-199)
מִסְפָּר	b.	number (100-199)
סֹפֵר	c.	scribe (54)
עזב	**40**	to leave, abandon
פנה	**41**	to turn about
פָּנֶה* <לִפְנֵי	a.	face (over 500); (prep.) before
פֶּן (?)	b.	lest (100-199)
פְּנִימִי	c.	the inner (32, 24 in Ezek.)
פִּנָּה	d.	corner (29)
פְּנִימָה	e.	within (13)
פתח (1)[1]	**42**	to open; to loosen, free (Pi.)
פֶּתַח	a.	gate, opening, entrance (100-199)
קבץ	**43**	to assemble, gather together
קבר	**44**	to bury
קֶבֶר	a.	grave (67)
קְבוּרָה	b.	burial, grave (14)
קדשׁ	**45**	to be holy; to consecrate (Pi.)
קֹדֶשׁ	a.	holy (thing) (300-500)
קָדוֹשׁ	b.	holy (100-199)
מִקְדָּשׁ	c.	sanctuary (70-99)
קטר	**46**	to send an offering up in smoke (Pi.); to make smoke (Hi.)
קְטֹרֶת	a.	incense (70-99, 41 in Ex.-Num.)
קרב	**47**	to draw near
קֶרֶב	a.	inward part; midst (200-299)
קָרוֹב, (f.) קְר	b.	near (70-99)
קָרְבָּן	c.	offering, gift (70-99, 78 in Lev.-Num.)
קָרֵב	d.	near (11)
רדף	**48**	to pursue, persecute

[1] For פתח (2), see p. 31, no. 177

רום	**49**	to be high, exalted
תְּרוּמָה	a.	heave-offering (70-99)
מָרוֹם	b.	height, high (54)
רוץ	**50**	to run
רעה (1)[1]	**51**	to feed, graze, tend (cattle)
רֹעֶה		Qal ptc.: shepherd
מִרְעֶה	a.	pasture (13)
מַרְעִית	b.	pasturing (10)
שׂמח	**52**	to rejoice; to gladden (Pi.)
שִׂמְחָה	a.	rejoicing (70-99)
שָׂמֵחַ	b.	joyful (21)
שׂנא	**53**	to hate
שֹׂנֵא, *מְשַׂנֵּא		(Qal & Pi. ptc.: adversary, enemy)
שִׂנְאָה	a.	hatred (17)
שׂרף	**54**	to burn
שְׂרֵפָה	a.	burning (13)
שׁאל	**55**	to ask
שָׁאוּל	a.	Saul (300-500)
שְׁאֵלָה	b.	request (14)
שׁאר	**56**	to remain, be left over (Ni., Hi.)
שְׁאֵרִית	a.	rest, remainder (67)
שְׁאָר	b.	remnant (25)
שׁבע	**57**	to swear (Ni., Hi.)
שֶׁבַע	a.	seven (300-500)
שִׁבְעִים	b.	seventy (70-99)
שְׁבִיעִי	c.	seventh (70-99)
שְׁבוּעָה	d.	oath (31)
שָׁבוּעַ	e.	week (20)
שׁבר (1)[2]	**58**	to break; to shatter (Pi.)
שֶׁבֶר, שֵׁבֶר (1)[3]	a.	breaking, destruction (42)
שׁחת	**59**	to spoil, ruin (Pi.); to be corrupt, spoiled (Ni.); to destroy (Hi.)
מַשְׁחִית	a.	destroyer, destruction (36)
שׁכח	**60**	to forget
שׁכן	**61**	to tent, dwell, settle

[1] For רעה (2), see p. 26, no. 36

[2] For שׁבר (2), see p. 18, no. 95

[3] For שֶׁבֶר (2), see p. 18, no. 95a

מִשְׁכָּן a. dwelling, tabernacle (100-199)

שָׁכֵן b. inhabitant (20)

שׁלך **62** to throw, cast (Hi.)

שׁלם **63** to be whole, complete;
to repay, recompense (Pi.);
to make peace with or live in peace with (Hi.)

שָׁלוֹם a. peace (200-299)

שְׁלֹמֹה b. Solomon (100-199)

שֶׁלֶם c. final or peace offering (70-99, 49 in Lev.-Num.)

שָׁלֵם d. whole, perfect (27)

שׁפך **64** to pour out

I D. Verbs Occurring 70-99 Times

אסר **1** to bind

אָסִיר , אַסִּיר a. prisoner (15)

אֵסָר, אִסָּר b. fetter, bond (11)

מוֹסֵר c. bands (11)

† (1) בער **2** to consume, burn

הפך **3** to turn, overturn

תַּהְפֻּכוֹת a. perversity, deceit (10, 9 in Prov., 1 in Deut. 32 : 20)

† (1) זנה **4** to commit fornication, play the harlot

תַּזְנוּת a. fornication (22, all in Ezek. 16 and 23)

זְנוּנִים b. fornication (11)

זְנוּת c. fornication (9)

זעק[1] **5** to cry out

זְעָקָה a. cry (18)

חלה **6** to be weak, sick;
to soften, put in gentle mood (Pi.)

חֳלִי a. sickness (24)

† (1) חנן **7** to be gracious, favor;
to implore favor or compassion (Hith.)

חֵן a. grace, favor (69)

חִנָּם b. gratis, in vain, without reason (32)

תְּחִנָּה c. supplication (25)

תַּחֲנוּנִים d. supplication(s) (18)

חַנּוּן e. gracious (13)

† (1) חפץ (Qal) **8** to please, delight

חֵפֶץ a. delight (39)

† (1) חרה **9** to become hot, burning, angry

חָרוֹן a. burning, anger (41)

טהר **10** to be clean (44 t. in Lev.)

טָהוֹר a. clean (70-99, 49 in Ex.-Lev.)

טָהֳרָה b. cultic purification (13, 8 in Lev.)

[1] Cf. with I E. 37 below

טוב **11** to be good, pleasant

טוֹב a. good (300-500)

טוֹבָה b. good things, fortune (100-199)

טוּב c. good things, wealth (31)

יעץ **12** to give counsel, advise

† (1) עֵצָה a. counsel (70-99)

לין **13** to spend the night, lodge

למד **14** to learn;
to teach (Pi.)

† (1) מאס **15** to reject

מכר **16** to sell

מִמְכָּר a. merchandise; sale (10, 7 in Lev. 25)

† (1) מלט **17** to escape, save, deliver

משח **18** to anoint

מָשִׁיחַ a. anointed one (39)

(1-2) מִשְׁחָה b. anointing; portion (23, all but one in Ex., Lev.)

(2)[1] משל (Qal) **19** to rule

מֶמְשָׁלָה a. dominion (16)

נבט **20** to look at, regard (Hi.)

נצב **21** to take one's stand, be stationed (Ni.)
to set up, erect, place (Hi.)

מַצֵּבָה a. pillar (32)

נְצִיב b. garrison; pillar (12)

מַצָּב c. station, garrison (10)

סגר **22** to shut, close upon;
to deliver up, give in one's power (Hi.)

מִסְגֶּרֶת a. bulwark, rim (17)

סתר **23** to conceal, hide (Ni., Hi.)

סֵתֶר a. hiding place, secrecy (35)

[1] For משל (1), see p. 17, no. 32

מִסְתָּר	b.	hiding place (10)
עוּר (3)[1]	**24**	to arouse, awake
עזר	**25**	to help, assist
עֶזְרָה	a.	help, assistance (26)
עֵזֶר	b.	helper; succor (21)
ענה (2)[2]	**26**	to be afflicted, humble; to oppress, humiliate (Pi.)
עָנִי	a.	afflicted, poor (70-99)
עֳנִי	b.	poverty, affliction (36)
עָנָו	c.	poor, humble, meek (21)
ערך	**27**	to arrange, set in order
עֵרֶךְ	a.	order (33, 24 in Lev.)
מַעֲרֶכֶת	b.	row, layer (17)
מַעֲרָכָה	c.	battle array (12)
פלא	**28**	to be extraordinary, wonderful (Ni., Hi.)
פֶּלֶא	a.	wonder (13)
פלל (2) †	**29**	to pray (Hith.)
תְּפִלָּה	a.	prayer (70-99)
קלל	**30**	to be slight, trifling, swift; to declare cursed (Pi.); to make light, treat with contempt (Hi.)
קְלָלָה	a.	curse (33)
קנה (1) †	**31**	to acquire, buy
מִקְנֶה	a.	possession (of land, cattle) (70-99)
קִנְיָן	b.	(individual) property; flock, goods (10)
רחץ	**32**	to wash
רכב	**33**	to ride
רֶכֶב	a.	chariotry (100-199)
מֶרְכָּבָה	b.	chariot (44)
רעע (1) †	**34**	to be wicked, evil
רָעָה	a.	evil (300-500)
רַע	b.	evil (200-299)
רֹעַ	c.	wickedness (19)
שׂבע	**35**	to satisfy, be sated with
שָׂבֵעַ	a.	sated, satisfied (10)
שׂכל	**36**	to have insight, comprehension; to prosper (Hi.)
שֵׂכֶל, שֶׂכֶל	a.	insight, prudence (16)
שׁבת	**37**	to cease, rest
שַׁבָּת	a.	sabbath (100-199)
שַׁבָּתוֹן	b.	sabbatical observance (11, 8 in Lev.)
שׁחט (1) †	**38**	to slaughter, kill
שׁיר (שָׁר, מְשׁוֹרֵר)	**39**	to sing (Qal and Polel ptc.: singer)
שִׁיר	a.	song (70-99)
שִׁירָה	b.	song (14)
שׁית (Qal)	**40**	to put, place
שׁמד	**41**	to destroy, exterminate (Ni., Hi.)
שׁמם	**42**	to be astonished; to be desolate
שְׁמָמָה	a.	desolation, waste (57)
שַׁמָּה	b.	astonishment, desolation (39)
שׁקה	**43**	to give to drink (Hi.)
שׁרת	**44**	to minister unto, serve (Pi.)

I E. Verbs Occurring 69-50 Times

תקע	**1**	to clap; blow (the trumpet) (68)
אחז	**2**	to seize, grasp (67)
אֲחֻזָּה	a.	landed property, possession (65)
פוץ	**3**	to spread, disperse, scatter (67)
פרשׂ	**4**	to spread out (67)
רפא	**5**	to heal (67)
מַרְפֵּא	a.	healing, health (13)
רְפָאִים (1,2)	b.	Rephaim (10); dead men, shades (8)
ריב	**6**	to strive, contend, conduct a legal case or suit (66)
רִיב	a.	strife, case at law (62)
שׁכם (den.)	**7**	to rise early (Hi.) (66)
שְׁכֶם	a.	shoulders (22)
ברח	**8**	to flee, run away; to chase away (Hi.) (65)
בְּרִיחַ	a.	bar (44)
כשׁל	**9**	to stumble (65)
מִכְשׁוֹל	a.	stumbling-block (14)
מהר (1) †	**10**	to hasten (Pi.) (65)

[1] For עור (1), see p. 29, no. 96;
עור (2), see p. 27, no. 45

[2] For ענה (1), see p. 5, no. 29;
ענה (3), see p. 25, no. 13;
ענה (4), see p. 20, no. 190

מְהֵרָה a. quickly (20)

מַהֵר b. hastily, quickly (18)

נצח **11** to act as overseer, director of (Pi.); to be enduring (Ni.) (65, as Pi. ptc. in vs. 1 of 55 Ps.)

† (1) נֵצַח a. eminence, glory; forever; as negative: never (43)

צלח **12** to be successful, prosper (65)

תפש **13** to catch, seize (64)

ארר **14** to curse (63)

† (2) אורים (?) a. Urim (8)

יצר **15** to form (63, 21 in Is. 40-55)

יֵצֶר a. form, purpose (9)

קרע **16** to tear, rend (63)

תמם **17** to be complete; to be consumed, exhausted, spent (63)

תָּמִים a. perfect, complete (70-99)

תֹּם b. completeness (28)

תָּם c. whole, complete (15)

נצר (Qal) **18** to watch, keep guard (62)

יבשׁ **19** to become dry, wither (61)

יַבָּשָׁה a. dry land (14)

נטע **20** to plant (60)

יכח **21** to reprove (Hi.) (59)

תּוֹכַחַת a. reproof (24, 16 in Prov.)

נחל **22** to inherit, take possession of (59)

נַחֲלָה a. inheritance (200-299)

חדל (Qal) **23** to cease (58)

פדה **24** to redeem, ransom (58)

שׁדד **25** to devastate, despoil (58)

† (2) שֹׁד a. violence, devastation (25)

חלק **26** to divide, apportion (57)

חֵלֶק a. lot, portion (66)

מַחֲלֹקֶת b. share (of property), division, group (41, 36 in Chr.)

חֶלְקָה c. plot of land, field (23)

רחק **27** to be remote; to remove (Hi.) (57)

רָחוֹק a. far, distant (70-99)

מֶרְחָק b. far off (18)

זרע **28** to sow (56)

זֶרַע a. seed (200-299)

פעל (Qal) **29** to do, make (56)

פֹּעַל a. deed (38)

פְּעֻלָּה b. wages, work (14)

† (1) רצה **30** to be pleased, favorable (56)

רָצוֹן a. pleasure, desire (56)

חזה (Qal) **31** to see, gaze at (55)

חָזוֹן a. vision (34)

חֹזֶה b. seer (17)

חִזָּיוֹן c. vision (9)

חתת **32** to be shattered, terrified, disheartened (55)

מְחִתָּה a. ruin (11)

יצק **33** to pour out (55)

אבה (Qal) **34** to be willing (54)

(?) אֶבְיוֹן (#) a. needy (61)

דבק **35** to cleave, cling (54)

כעס **36** to be discontent; to grieve, offend (Hi.) (54)

כַּעַס a. vexation (21)

צעק[1] **37** to cry out, summon (54)

צְעָקָה a. cry, lamentation (21)

רנן **38** to jubilate, cry for joy (54)

רִנָּה a. cry of joy or entreaty (33)

ברא (1)[2] **39** to create (53)

מדד **40** to measure (53, 36 in Ezek. 40-47)

† (1) מִדָּה a. measure (55, 26 in Ezek. 40-47)

מַד* b. cloth, garment (12)

ירה (3)[3] (den.) **41** to direct, instruct (Hi.) (52)

תּוֹרָה a. teaching, law (200-299)

נדח **42** to scatter (52)

בקע **43** to cleave, split, burst upon (51)

בִּקְעָה a. valley, plain (20)

חרם (den.) **44** to destroy, devote, banish (Hi.) (51)

† (1) חֵרֶם, חֶרֶם a. thing or person devoted (29)

כבס **45** to wash (Pi.) (51, 31 in Lev.)

פרץ **46** to break, break through (51)

פֶּרֶץ a. breach (19)

בגד **47** to deal treacherously with (50)

[1] Cf. with I D. 5 above

[2] For ברא (2), see p. 30, no. 159

[3] For ירה (1), see p. 14, no. 117

בֶּגֶד	a.	garment (200-299)
נכר	48	to make unrecognizable, be strange (Pi., Hith.) to inspect, acknowledge, know (Hi.) (50)
נָכְרִי	a.	foreign,alien (46)
נֵכָר	b.	foreigner (36)
נשׂג	49	to reach, overtake (Hi.) (50)
תעה	50	to err, go astray, stagger, become confused (50)

I F. Verbs Occurring 49-25 Times

מנה	1	to count; to appoint (Pi.) (29)
מִן(?)	a.	(prep.) from, out of, part of; (conj.) since, than (in comparisons), on account of (over 500)
מָנָה	b.	portion, part (13)
עוד	2	to admonish, take as witness, bear witness (Hi.) (45)
עוֹד	a.	yet, still, again (over 500)
עֵד, עֵדָה (f.)	b.	witness (70-99)
עֵדוּת	c.	sign of reminder, testimony (61)
שׁנה	3	to change, repeat (26)
שְׁנַיִם	a.	two (over 500)
שָׁנָה	b.	year (over 500)
שֵׁנִי	c.	second (100-199)
מִשְׁנֶה	d.	second, double, copy (35)
צדק	4	to be in the right; to do justice, pronounce or treat as just (Hi.) (41)
צַדִּיק	a.	righteous, just (200-299)
צֶדֶק	b.	righteousness (100-199)
צְדָקָה	c.	righteousness (100-199)
יעד	5	to appoint, designate (29)
מוֹעֵד	a.	appointed place or time; season (200-299)
עֵדָה	b.	congregation (100-199)
רגל (den.)	6	to spy out, slander (Pi.) (26)
רֶגֶל	a.	foot (200-299)
רשׁע	7	to be guilty; to live in wickedness, act guilty, condemn as guilty (Hi.) (35)
רָשָׁע	a.	guilty, wicked (one) (200-299)
רֶשַׁע, רִשְׁעָה (f.)	b.	wrong, wickedness, guilt (43)
אור	8	to be light; to shine (Hi.) (43)
אוֹר	a.	light (100-199)
מָאוֹר	b.	luminary (19)
אזן (den.)	9	to listen to, heed (Hi.) (43)
אֹזֶן	a.	ear (100-199)
גבר	10	to be superior over, prevail (25)
גִּבּוֹר	a.	mighty man, warrior (100-199)
גֶּבֶר	b.	vigorous young man (65)
גְּבוּרָה	c.	strength, strong performance (of God) (62)
גְּבִירָה, (גְּבֶרֶת)	d.	mistress, lady, queen-mother (17)
גרשׁ	11	to drive out or away (47)
מִגְרָשׁ	a.	pasture or untilled ground (100-199, 95 in Josh.-I Chr.)
המה (Qal)	12	to make noise, be tumultuous (33)
הָמוֹן	a.	tumult, turmoil, multitude (70-99)
זקן	13	to be old (28)
(den. of זָקֵן)		
זָקֵן	a.	old (100-199)
זָקָן	b.	beard (19)
חכם	14	to be wise (27, 13 in Prov.)
חָכָם	a.	skilful, wise (100-199)
חָכְמָה	b.	experience, shrewdness, wisdom (100-199)
ישׁר	15	to be straight, right, smooth (27)
יָשָׁר	a.	straight, right, upright (100-199)
מִישׁוֹר	b.	plain, level, uprightness (23)
מֵישָׁרִים	c.	upright(ness),evenness, equity (19)
יֹשֶׁר	d.	straightness, uprightness (14)
פרה	16	to be fruitful (29, 15 in Gen.)
פְּרִי	a.	fruit (100-199)
צפה (1)[1]	17	to watch, spy, look out (37)
צָפוֹן	a.	north (100-199)
קהל (den.)	18	to assemble, summon (Ni., Hi.) (39)
קָהָל	a.	assembly, congregation (100-199)

[1] For צפה (2), see p. 13, no. 51

קרה (קרא [2] 6 t.)[1]	**19**	to meet, befall (28)
(לִקְרַאת)		(Qal inf. > prep., over against, opposite [100-199])
קִרְיָה	a.	place, town (29)
מִקְרֶה	b.	accident, chance, fortune (10)
רחב	**20**	to expand; to enlarge (Hi.) (25)
רֹחַב	a.	breadth (100-199, 54 in Ezek. 40-48)
רְחוֹב	b.	open place (of town) (43)
רָחָב	c.	broad, wide, large (21)
ארך	**21**	to be long; to lengthen (Hi.) (34)
אֹרֶךְ	a.	length (70-99)
אָרֵךְ*	b.	long (15)
דין	**22**	to plead one's cause, judge (25)
דָּן	a.	Dan (70-99)
מְדִינָה	b.	district of jurisdiction, province, satrapy (43, 29 in Es.)
מָדוֹן	c.	strife (23, 19 in Prov.)
דִּין	d.	legal case, judgment (19)
חרף (2) †	**23**	to taunt, reproach (40)
חֶרְפָּה	a.	reproach, disgrace (70-99)
עוף	**24**	to fly (27)
עוֹף	a.	flying creatures: fowl, insects (70-99)
עַפְעַפַּיִם *	b.	eyelashes (10)
פשע	**25**	to rebel, revolt against (41)
פֶּשַׁע	a.	rebellion, revolt, transgression (70-99)
צרר (1)	**26**	to be in distress; be narrow; wrap, shut up (34)
צָרָה	a.	distress (70-99)
צַר (1)	b.	narrow; distress, dismay (38)
צרר (2) (Qal)	**27**	to show hostility toward (27)
צַר (2)	a.	adversary, foe (70-99)
קדם	**28**	to be in front, do beforehand (Pi.) (26)
קָדִים, קָדִימָה	a.	east, eastward (69)
קֶדֶם	b.	before; east (61)
קֵדְמָה (< קֵדֶם*)	c.	eastward (26)
קַדְמוֹנִי קַדְמֹנִיּוֹת (f. plu.),	d.	eastern; ancient one (10)
חלם	**29**	to dream (26)
חֲלוֹם	a.	dream (64, 34 in Gen.)

[1] For קרא (1), see p. 4, no. 22

נסך (1) †	**30**	to consecrate (by pouring libations); to pour out, offer (libation) (Hi.) (25)
נֶסֶךְ, נֵסֶךְ	a.	libation (64, 33 in Num.)
מַסֵּכָה (1) †	b.	molten image (26)
נדר (Qal)	**31**	to vow (31)
נֶדֶר	a.	vow (60)
זמר (1) †	**32**	to sing, praise (Pi.) (43, 39 in Ps.)
מִזְמוֹר	a.	psalm (57, in vs. 1 of 57 Ps.)
שבה	**33**	to take captive (47)
שְׁבִי, שִׁבְיָה (f.)	a.	captive (56)
שְׁבוּת	b.	captivity (32)
קצר (1)[1] (Qal)	**34**	to reap (35)
קָצִיר	a.	harvest (54)
יסר	**35**	to admonish, correct, discipline (42)
מוּסָר	a.	chastening, discipline (50, 30 in Prov.)
נבל	**36**	to wither, fade; to treat with contumely (Pi.) (25)
נְבֵלָה	a.	corpse (49)
נֵבֶל (#) (?)	b.	harp (38)
נָבָל	c.	stupid, impious (18)
נְבָלָה	d.	senselessness, folly (13)
נגף	**37**	to smite, plague (49)
מַגֵּפָה	a.	plague (26)
פרר (1) †	**38**	to break, destroy, frustrate, invalidate (Hi.) (49)
קוה (1) †	**39**	to wait for, expect (49)
תִּקְוָה	a.	hope, expectation (34)
קַו (1) †	b.	measuring line (19)
סמך	**40**	to support, lay one's hands on (48)
פחד	**41**	to fear, tremble (25)
פַּחַד	a.	trembling, dread (48)
חרשׁ (2)[2]	**42**	to be silent (Hi.) (47)
חֵרֵשׁ	a.	deaf (9)
יצב	**43**	to stand firmly (Hith.) (47)
רחם	**44**	to have compassion, mercy (47)
רַחֲמִים	a.	mercies (39)
רֶחֶם	b.	womb (25)
רַחוּם	c.	compassionate (13)

[1] For קצר (2), see p. 20, no. 163

[2] For חרשׁ (1), see p. 14, no. 116

רצח	**45**	to kill (47)
אשם	**46**	to do wrong, be guilty (36)
אָשָׁם	a.	guilt, guilt-offering (46, 28 in Lev.)
אַשְׁמָה	b.	guilt (18)
† (1) בלע	**47**	to swallow (46)
סלח	**48**	to forgive (46)
עצר	**49**	to detain, restrain, retain (46)
פגע	**50**	to meet, light upon, fall upon, encounter (with hostility); entreat (46)
[1] (2) צפה	**51**	to overlay, plate (Pi.) (46)
קשב	**52**	to give attention to (Hi.) (46)
גיל (Qal)	**53**	to rejoice, triumph over (45)
גִּיל	a.	exultant shout, rejoicing (10)
מרה	**54**	to be disobedient, rebellious (45)
מְרִי	a.	rebellion (23, 16 in Ezek.)
רפה	**55**	to sink down, drop, weaken; to abandon, forsake (Hi.) (45)
חגר (Qal)	**56**	to gird (44)
(חול) חיל (1) [2]	**57**	to be in labor-pain, to tremble (44)
חלץ	**58**	to draw off, strip; be equipped for war (44)
קשר	**59**	to tie together, conspire (44)
קֶשֶׁר	a.	conspiracy (14)
רוע	**60**	to shout (Hi.) (44)
תְּרוּעָה	a.	shout (36)
בזה	**61**	to despise (43)
הרה	**62**	to conceive, become pregnant (43)
הָרָה	a.	pregnant (15)
הרס	**63**	to tear or throw down (43)
יסד	**64**	to found, establish (43)
יְסוֹד	a.	foundation (20)
(f.), מוּסָד	b.	foundation (13)
נוע	**65**	to quiver, move unsteadily (43)
נקה	**66**	to be clean, innocent, free from guilt (Ni.); to leave unpunished, acquit (Pi.) (41)
נָקִיא, נָקִי	a.	exempt, free from guilt, innocent (43)
פשט	**67**	to strip or put off, make a dash for or against (43)

[1] For צפה (1), see p. 11, no. 17

[2] For חיל (2), see p. 26, no. 22

קנא	**68**	to be jealous, zealous (Pi., Hi.) (34)
קִנְאָה	a.	ardor, passion, jealousy (43)
בדל	**69**	to separate, divide (Ni., Hi.) (42)
בזז	**70**	to plunder (42)
בַּז	a.	booty (26)
בִּזָּה	b.	spoil (10)
בלל	**71**	to mix, moisten, confound (42)
זוב (Qal)	**72**	to flow (42)
† (1) זרה	**73**	to scatter, winnow (42)
† (1) חרב	**74**	to be dried up, desolate (37)
חָרְבָּה	a.	desolate place, ruin (42)
חֹרֶב	b.	dryness, desolation (17)
חָרֵב	c.	dry, waste, desolate (10)
נתץ	**75**	to pull down, break (42)
אמץ	**76**	to be strong, prevail; to strengthen (Pi.) (41)
ארב	**77**	to lie in ambush (41)
חמל (Qal)	**78**	to have compassion on, spare (41)
יחל	**79**	to wait (Pi.); to tarry (Hi.) (41)
מאן	**80**	to refuse (Pi.) (41)
מוט	**81**	to totter, reel, stagger (41, 27 in Ps.)
מוֹטָה	a.	bar, yoke (12)
רגז	**82**	to quake, disturb, excite (41)
נטש	**83**	to leave, forsake, abandon (40)
[1] (1) אבל	**84**	to mourn (39)
(אָבֵל) אֵבֶל	a.	mourning rites, funeral ceremony (24)
בהל	**85**	to be terrified, disturbed (Ni.); to terrify, dismay (Pi.) (39)
גנב	**86**	to steal (39)
גַּנָּב	a.	thief (17)
חרד	**87**	to tremble; to disturb (Hi.) (39)
† (1) נחה	**88**	to lead, guide (39)
גבה	**89**	to be high, exalted (35)
גָּבֹהַּ	a.	high (38)
גֹּבַהּ	b.	height (17)
חבא	**90**	to hide (Ni., Hith.) (38)
כלם	**91**	to be humiliated, put to shame (Ni.); to molest, insult (Hi.) (38)

[1] For אבל (2), see p. 28, no. 74

כְּלִמָּה	a.	insult (30)
שׁקט	92	to be undisturbed, quiet (38)
בצר (3) †	93	to be unapproachable, impossible (Ni.); to make inaccessible (Pi.) (28)
(בָּצוּר)		(Qal pass. ptc.: fortified, inaccessible, 25)
מִבְצָר	a.	fortified city (37)
חסה (Qal)	94	to seek refuge (37)
מַחְסֶה	a.	refuge (20)
כול	95	to contain, hold in (Hi.); to supply (Pilpel) (37)
לקט	96	to glean, gather (37)
נוף (1) †	97	to move to and fro, swing, wield (Hi.) (37)
תְּנוּפָה	a.	wave-offering (30)
עשׁק	98	to oppress, wrong (37)
עֹשֶׁק, עֲשֻׁקָה (f.)	a.	oppression (16)
כרע	99	to kneel, bow down (36)
משׁך	100	to draw, drag; to be prolonged, postponed (Ni.) (36)
נסה	101	to test, try (Pi.) (36)
פרח (Qal)	102	to sprout, blossom, break forth (36)
פֶּרַח	a.	bud, blossom (15)
קשׁה	103	to be hard, difficult, stubborn (Hi.) (28)
קָשֶׁה	a.	hard, difficult (36)
כנע	104	to be subdued, humbled (Ni., Hi.) (35, 17 in Chr.)
מול (1) †	105	to circumcise (35)
מעל (Qal)	106	to be unfaithful (35)
מַעַל (1)[1]	a.	unfaithfulness, disloyalty (29)
נקם	107	to take vengeance, avenge (35)
נְקָמָה	a.	vengeance (26)
נָקָם	b.	vengeance (17)
שׂחק[2]	108	to play, laugh (35)
שְׂחוֹק	a.	laughter, derision (16)
זרק (1) †	109	to sprinkle (34)
מִזְרָק	a.	bowl (32, 15 in Num.)
יהב	110	to give (Qal imp. int. formation) (34)
(הָבוּ, הָבִי, הָבָה, הַב)		

[1] For מַעַל (2), see p. 3, no. 17c

[2] Cf. צחק on p. 16, no. 15

מחה (1) †	111	to wipe off, blot out (34)
צפן	112	to hide, treasure up (34)
צרף	113	to smelt, refine (34)
קצף	114	to be wroth, angry (34)
קֶצֶף	a.	wrath (29)
חבשׁ	115	to bind, gird (33)
חרשׁ (1)[1]	116	to plow, engrave, devise (27)
חָרָשׁ (2) †	a.	craftsman, engraver (33)
ירה (1)[2]	117	to cast, shoot (33)
צור (1) †	118	to bind, besiege (30)
מָצוֹר, מְצוּרָה (f.),	a.	siege (33)
צמח	119	to sprout, spring up, grow (33)
חתן (den.)	120	to be an in-law, marry (32)
(חֹתֵן)		(Qal ptc. 15 t. in Ex.)
חָתָן	a.	son-in-law, bridegroom (20)
ילל	121	to howl, wail (Hi.) (32)
כחד	122	to hide (Ni., Pi.); to efface (Hi.) (32)
נשׁק (1)[3]	123	to kiss (32)
דמה (1)[4]	124	to be like, resemble; to liken (Pi.) (31)
דְּמוּת	a.	likeness, pattern (24, 14 in Ezek.)
טמן	125	to hide (31)
יצת	126	to burn, kindle (31)
נאף	127	to commit adultery (31)
סכך	128	to block, make unapproachabl (26)
סֻכָּה	a.	covert of foliage (31)
מָסָךְ	b.	covering, screen (25, 16 in E
שׁטף	129	to wash off, flood, overflow (3
בחן	130	to try, prove, examine (30)
גזל	131	to tear away, plunder (30)
דמם	132	to be silent, motionless (30)
נהג (1) †	133	to lead, drive (30)
ספד	134	to lament, wail (30)
מִסְפֵּד	a.	lamentation (16)

[1] For חרשׁ (2), see p. 12, no. 42

[2] For ירה (3), see p. 10, no. 41

[3] For נשׁק (2), see p. 31, no. 186

[4] For דמה (2), see p. 20, no. 168

רבץ	135	to lie down (30)
† (1) רעשׁ	136	to quake, shake (30)
רַעַשׁ	a.	quaking, rustling, rattling (17)
תלה	137	to hang (30)
חמם	138	to be warm, hot, inflamed (29)
חַמָּה	a.	heat, glow; sun (6)
מנע	139	to withhold (29)
בשׁל	140	to boil (28)
† (2) חבר	141	to join, associate (28, 14 in Ex.)
חָבֵר	a.	companion (13)
† (1) חלף	142	to pass on, over, away; to renew, change (28)
חֲלִיפָה	a.	change, substitute, relief (11)
חשׂך	143	to withhold, keep back (28)
ליץ (לוץ)	144	to deride; to be spokesman, interpreter (Hi.) (28, 18 in Prov.)
(לֵץ)		(Qal ptc.: prattler, scorner, 15 t.)
עלם	145	to hide, conceal (28)
פלט	146	to escape, bring into security (Pi.) (27)
פְּלֵיטָה	a.	escape (28)
פָּלִיט	b.	escaped one, fugitive (19)
פ (1) † (den.)	147	to be simple, susceptible to deception, deceive (28)
פֶּתִי	a.	simple youth (19, 15 in Prov.)
שׁפל	148	to be low; to lay low, abase, humiliate (Hi.) (28)
שְׁפֵלָה	a.	lowland (20)
שָׁפָל	b.	low (19)
חקר	149	to search through, explore (27)
חֵקֶר	a.	searching (12)
חתם (den.)	150	to seal (27)
חוֹתָם	a.	seal (14)
נדד	151	to flee, wander, run away (27)
נתק	152	to pull off; to tear apart (Pi.); to separate (Ni.) (27)
נֶתֶק	a.	scab (14, Lev.)
שׂושׂ (Qal)	153	to rejoice (27)
שָׂשׂוֹן	a.	joy (22)
מָשׂוֹשׂ	b.	joy (17)
אוה	154	to long or wish for (Pi., Hith.) (26)
תַּאֲוָה	a.	desire (20)
יגע	155	to grow weary, toil (26)
* יְגִיעַ	a.	toil, labor; product, acquired property (16)
פרד	156	to separate, divide (26)
פֶּרֶד	a.	mule (15)
אפה	157	to bake (25)
† (1) הגה	158	to meditate, mutter (25)
חצב	159	to hew, hew out (25)
טרף	160	to tear, rend (25)
טֶרֶף	a.	prey, food (22)
טְרֵפָה	b.	thing torn (9)
† (1) ישׁן	161	to sleep (25)
שֵׁנָה	a.	sleep (23)
מרד (Qal)	162	to rebel, revolt (25)
שׁלף (Qal)	163	to draw, tear out (25)
תור	164	to spy out, explore (25)

I G. Verbs Occurring 24-10 Times

אחר	1	to hesitate, tarry, detain, keep back (Pi.) (18)
אַחַר	a.	(prep.) behind, after (over 500)
אַחֵר	b.	another (100-199)
אַחֲרִית	c.	end, last (61)
מָחָר	d.	tomorrow (52)
אַחֲרוֹן	e.	at the back, last (51)
אָחוֹר	f.	behind, west (41)
מָחֳרָת	g.	the next day, the morrow (32)
כהן (den. of כֹּהֵן)	2	to be a priest (23, 12 in Ex.)
כֹּהֵן	a.	priest (over 500)
כְּהֻנָּה	b.	priesthood (14)
צבא	3	to wage war; to muster (Hi.) (14)
† (1) צָבָא	a.	service in war, host, army (300-500)
† (1) רבב	4	to be many, manifold, much (22)

רַב a. much, many (300-500)

רֹב b. multitude, abundance (100-199)

רְבָבָה c. very large multitude, myriad, ten thousand (16)

רבע (2) † **5** to have four corners, be squared (12)

(den. of אַרְבַּע)

אַרְבַּע a. four (300-500)

אַרְבָּעִים b. forty (100-199)

רְבִיעִי c. fourth (56)

רוח **6** to perceive, smell (Hi.) (11)

רוּחַ a. spirit, wind (300-500)

רֵיחַ b. scent, odor (58, 35 in Lev.-Num.)

אנף (Qal) **7** to be angry (14)

אַף (2)[1] a. nose, nostril, anger (200-299)

חדשׁ **8** to renew (Pi.) (10)

חֹדֶשׁ a. new moon, month (200-299)

חָדָשׁ b. new, recent, fresh (54)

עוה **9** to do wrong;
to be bewildered, disconcerted (Ni.)
to pervert (Hi.) (17)

עָוֺן a. transgression, iniquity (200-299)

בלה **10** to be worn out;
to consume away, use to the full (Pi.) (16)

בִּלְתִּי a. not, beside (100-199)

בַּל b. negation, non-existence, not (66, 31 in Ps.)

בְּלִי c. without (55)

בְּלִיַּעַל d. wicked, wickedness (27)

בִּלְעֲדֵי*,

בַּלְעֲדֵי e. apart from, besides (17)

(?) אֲבָל (#) f. verily, alas! (11)

חצה **11** to divide (15)

חֲצִי a. half (100-199)

מַחֲצִית b. half (16)

חקק **12** to engrave, inscribe; enact, decree (19)

חֹק a. prescription, rule (100-199)

חֻקָּה b. statute, prescription (100-199)

מעט **13** to become few;
to diminish (Hi.) (22)

מְעַט a. fewness; a little (100-199)

[1] For אַף (1), see p. 36, III D. no. 5

עצם (1) † **14** to be strong, mighty, numerous (17)

עֶצֶם a. bone (100-199)

עָצוּם b. mighty (30)

צחק[1] **15** to laugh, sport, play (13)

יִצְחָק a. Isaac (100-199)

רעב **16** to be hungry (12)

רָעָב a. hunger, famine (100-199)

רָעֵב b. hungry (21)

תעב **17** to abhor, act abominably (Pi.) (22)

תּוֹעֵבָה a. abomination (100-199)

בעל (Qal) **18** to own, rule over (16)

בַּעַל a. owner, husband (70-99); Baal (70-99)

זרח (Qal) **19** to beam, shine forth (18)

מִזְרָח a. sunrise, east (70-99)

אֶזְרָח b. native (17)

חשׁך **20** to be or grow dark (18)

חֹשֶׁךְ a. darkness (70-99)

עזז **21** to be strong, prevail;
to show or appear with a defia
bold face (Hi.) (11)

עֹז (1)[2] a. strength, power, might (70-99

עֵז b. goat (70-99)

מָעוֹז c. strength (35)

עַז d. strong (23)

ענן **22** to cause to appear;
to practice soothsaying (Pi.) (1

עָנָן a. clouds (70-99)

שׁלל (2) † **23** to spoil, plunder (16)

שָׁלָל a. plunder, booty (70-99)

שׁקל **24** to weigh (22)

שֶׁקֶל a. shekel (70-99)

מִשְׁקָל b. weight (49)

חגג (Qal) **25** to keep a pilgrim feast, to ce
brate a day or feast (16)

חַג a. feast, procession (60)

עמל **26** to labor, toil (20)

עָמָל a. labor, trouble, misfortune (55

ערה **27** to uncover, pour out (Pi.) (14)

עֶרְוָה a. nakedness; pudenda (54, 31 Lev.)

עָרוֹם b. naked (16)

[1] Cf. with שׂחק, p. 14, no. 108

[2] For עֹז (2), see p. 30, 147a

תַּעַר c. knife, razor (13)
עֵירֹם d. nakedness (10)
טבע **28** to sink down (10)
טַבַּעַת a. signet-ring (49, 40 in Ex.)
† (2) פאר **29** to glorify (Pi., Hith.) (13)
תִּפְאֶרֶת a. glory, beauty, ornament (49)
גלל **30** to roll (18)
גִּלּוּלִים a. idols (48, 39 in Ezek.)
גַּל b. heap of stones; wave (of sea) (34)
מְגִלָּה c. roll of book, scroll (21)
גֻּלָּה d. bowl, basin (14)
גֻּלְגֹּלֶת e. skull (12)
גַּלְגַּל f. wheel (11)
בִּגְלַל g. (prep.) on account of, for the sake of (10)
[1] (1) עלל **31** to deal with ruthlessly; to glean (20)
*מַעֲלָל a. deeds, practices (42)
עֲלִילָה b. deed (24)
[2] (1) משל **32** to say a proverb; to be like (Ni.) (17)
מָשָׁל a. proverbial saying (39)
[3] (2) רמה **33** to deceive, beguile (Pi.) (12)
מִרְמָה a. deceit, treachery (39)
† (1) רְמִיָּה b. slackness, looseness; deceit (15)
מטר **34** to rain (Hi.) (17)
מָטָר a. rain (38)
מרר **35** to be bitter (15)
מַר a. bitter (37)
מֹר b. myrrh (12, 8 in Cant.)
עשׁר **36** to be rich (17)
עֹשֶׁר a. wealth (37)
עָשִׁיר b. rich, wealthy (23)
יקר **37** to be valued, precious (11)
יָקָר a. rare, precious (36)
יְקָרָה (f.),
יְקָר b. precious things; splendor, honor (17)
צרע **38** to be stricken with a skin disease (20)

צָרַעַת a. skin disease (35, 29 in Lev. 13-14)
אתה **39** to come (21)
אָתוֹן (?) a. female ass (34)
טבח (Qal) **40** to slaughter (11)
טַבָּח a. butcher, body-guard (33, 17 in Jer.)
טֶבַח b. slaughtering, slaughtered meat (16)
טִבְחָה (f.),
כזב **41** to lie, deceive (16)
כָּזָב a. lie (31)
צוד **42** to hunt, lie in wait for (16)
מָצָד a. place difficult to approach, fortress (29)
מְצוּדָה(2)(f.),
צַיִד b. hunting, game (19, 12 in Gen.)
צֵידָה c. provisions (10)
מָצוֹד d. hunting net, prey (9)
מְצוּדָה(1)(f.),
שׂכר **43** to hire (20)
שָׂכָר a. hire, wages (28)
שָׂכִיר b. hireling (18)
יקשׁ **44** to snare (10)
מוֹקֵשׁ a. snare, bait, lure (27)
סלל **45** to cast up, build a highway (10)
מְסִלָּה a. highway (27)
סֹלְלָה b. siege, assault-rampart (11)
נדב **46** to volunteer, offer freewill offerings (Hith.) (17)
נְדָבָה a. voluntary offering; free will (26)
נָדִיב b. willing; one who gives generously; noble one (26)
צום (Qal) **47** to fast (21)
צוֹם a. fast, time of fasting (25)
בשׂר **48** to announce, publish good news (Pi.) (24)
גוע (Qal) **49** to expire, perish, die (24)
חוס (Qal) **50** to be sorry, pity (24)
כבה **51** to be quenched, go out; to extinguish (Pi.) (24)
נאץ **52** to despise, contemn (24)
נזה **53** to sprinkle (Hi.) (24, 15 in Lev.)
נזר **54** to abstain, withdraw from (Ni.); to keep sacredly separate (Hi.) (12)

[1] For עלל (2), see p. 28, no. 71
[2] For משל (2), see p. 8, no. 19
[3] For רמה (1), see p. 28, no. 83

נֵזֶר a. consecration, diadem (24, 12 in Num. 6)

נָזִיר b. consecrated one, Nazirite (16)

סוג (1) † **55** to backslide, prove faithless; move back a boundary mark (24)

רדה (1) † (Qal) **56** to rule, dominate (24)

רושׁ **57** to be poor (24, 16 in Prov.)

שׁחר (2) † **58** to look or seek for (Pi.) (13)

שַׁחַר a. the reddish light preceding dawn, dawn (24)

שׁכל **59** to be bereaved of children; to make childless, suffer a miscarriage (Pi.) (24)

אֶשְׁכֹּל a. cluster of grapes; name of a valley near Hebron (13)

בצע **60** to cut off, finish (16)

בֶּצַע a. gain, profit (23)

גלח **61** to shave (Pi.) (23)

גמל **62** to deal fully, finish; to grow; do good or evil to (23)

גְּמוּל a. benefits (19)

חפר (1)[1] **63** to dig, search out (23)

חפשׂ **64** to search out (23)

יעל **65** to profit, benefit (Hi.) (23)

נגשׂ **66** to drive, press (23)

נקב **67** to bore, pierce, designate (23)

נְקֵבָה a. female (22, 12 in Lev.)

שׁכר **68** to drink, be drunk (19)

שֵׁכָר a. beer (23)

שִׁכּוֹר b. drunken (13)

גדע **69** to cut off, hew down (22)

גרע **70** to clip, diminish, withdraw (22)

זהר (2) † **71** to be mindful, warn (Ni., Hi.) (22), 16 in Ezek.)

זעם **72** to curse, scold (12)

זַעַם a. curse (22)

חושׁ **73** to make haste, act quickly (22)

חסר **74** to diminish, fail, lack (22)

חָסֵר a. one in want of, destitute (18, 13 in Prov.)

מַחְסוֹר b. want (13, 8 in Prov.)

ינק **75** to suckle, suck (22)

יוֹנֵק a. suckling (12)

כחשׁ **76** to deny, fail, lie (22)

[1] For חפר (2), see p. 19, no. 129

נפץ **77** to be scattered, dispersed; to dash to pieces (Pi.) (22, 12 i Jer.)

סקל **78** to stone (22)

ערב (1)[1] **79** to go surety for, pledge (22)

מַעֲרָב* (1)[2] a. articles of exchange (9, Ezek 27)

עתר **80** to entreat; to make supplication (Hi.) (22)

פשׂה (Qal) **81** to spread, be divulged (symptom of a disease) (22, Lev. 13-14)

קיץ **82** to awake (Hi.) (22)

שׁוע **83** to cry for help (Pi.) (22)

שַׁוְעָה a. cry for help (11)

שׁזר **84** to be twisted (Ho. ptc.) (22, Ex.

שׁען **85** to lean on, support oneself o (Ni.) (22)

מִשְׁעֶנֶת a. staff (11)

שׁקף **86** to look down upon (from above (Ni., Hi.) (22)

חמד **87** to desire (21)

חֶמְדָּה a. desirable things, pleasant (16)

מַחְמָד* b. desire (15)

חֲמֻדוֹת c. precious things (9, 6 in Da.)

מסס **88** to melt, become weak (Ni.) (21)

נתך **89** to pour out (21)

נתשׁ **90** to root out, pull up (21)

ספה **91** to sweep away, be consumed, destroyed (21)

פקח **92** to open the eyes (21)

פרס **93** to break bread; to have divided hoofs (Hi.) (14)

פַּרְסָה a. hoof (21)

שׁאג (Qal) **94** to roar (lion) (21)

שׁבר (2)[3] **95** to buy grain; to sell (Hi.) (21, 14 in Gen.)

שֶׁבֶר (2)[4] a. corn, grain (9, 6 in Gen.)

שׁגה **96** to err (inadvertently), commit si (ignorantly), swerve, go astray (21

שׁוה (1) † **97** to be like; to make smooth (Pi.) (21)

תמך **98** to grasp, lay hold of (21)

יחשׂ **99** to enroll oneself by genealogy (Hith.) (20, 15 in Chr.)

[1] For ערב (4), see p. 26, no. 34

[2] For מַעֲרָב (2), see p. 26, no. 34b

[3] For שׁבר (1), see p. 7, no. 58

[4] For שֶׁבֶר (1), see p. 7, no. 58a

ינה	**100**	to oppress (20)
מוּשׁ (2) †	**101**	to depart, be removed (20)
ערץ (Qal)	**102**	to suffer a shock, tremble (15)
עָרִיץ	a.	despot, tyrant; (the) ruthless (20)
קסם (Qal)	**103**	to practice divination (20)
קֶסֶם	a.	divination, decision (11)
שׂגב	**104**	to be high, inaccessible (20)
מִשְׂגָּב	a.	secure height, refuge (17)
שׂיח	**105**	to be concerned with a matter, consider (20, 14 in Prov.)
שִׂיחַ (2) †	a.	business, concern, talk (14)
ברר	**106**	to select, purify, be clean (19)
בַּר (3) †	a.	grain (14)
זמם (Qal)	**107**	to ponder, cogitate, purpose, devise (13)
מְזִמָּה	a.	purpose, device, evil thought (19)
נֶזֶם (?)	b.	ring; nose-or earring (17)
יאל (2) †	**108**	to show willingness, take it upon oneself to (Hi.) (19)
לאה	**109**	to be weary (19)
לחץ (Qal)	**110**	to squeeze, oppress, vex (19)
לַחַץ	a.	oppression (10)
עטה (1) †	**111**	to enwrap, cover (19)
ריק	**112**	to pour out, draw the sword (Hi.) (19)
רֵיקָם	a.	with empty hands; without success, property, cause (16)
רֵיק	b.	empty, vain (14)
רִיק	c.	empty, idle, worthless (12)
רצץ	**113**	to crush, oppress (19)
שׁאב (Qal)	**114**	to draw water (19)
דכא	**115**	to crush (Pi.) (18)
חבל (2) [1]	**116**	to seize as pledge (18)
יבל	**117**	to bring (Hi.) (18)
יְבוּל	a.	produce (of soil) (13)
כלא	**118**	to restrain, shut up (18)
כֶּלֶא	a.	prison (10)
לעג	**119**	to stutter, mock, deride (18)
נזל	**120**	to trickle, flow (18)
נטף	**121**	to drop, drip (18)
סות	**122**	to allure, incite (Hi.) (18)
סחר	**123**	to go about, trade, buy (18)

For חבל (3), see p. 20, no. 185

סרר (Qal)	**124**	to be stubborn, rebellious (18)
צמא (Qal)	**125**	to be thirsty (10)
צָמָא	a.	thirst (18)
צָמֵא	b.	thirsty (9)
רמס (Qal)	**126**	to tread, trample (18)
תכן	**127**	to estimate, adjust, mete out (18)
באשׁ	**128**	to stink, become odious (17)
חפר (2) [1]	**129**	to be ashamed, abashed (17)
כתת	**130**	to crush to pieces (17)
מוג	**131**	to melt, faint; to wave to and fro, swerve (Ni.); to dissolve (Polel) (17)
נקף (2) †	**132**	to go around, surround, enclose (Hi.) (17)
נשׁא (1)[2] (Qal)	**133**	to give a loan, lend (17)
סכן	**134**	to be of use or service (13)
Cf. סָגָן* (or סֶגֶן*)	a.	prefect, official, head (17)
עלז (Qal)	**135**	to rejoice, exult (17)
קדר	**136**	to be dark, dirty, in mourning attire (17)
רמשׂ (Qal)	**137**	to creep (17, 10 in Gen.)
רֶמֶשׂ	a.	small animals, creeping things (17, 10 in Gen.)
רקע	**138**	to stamp, beat out (11)
רָקִיעַ	a.	firmament (17, 9 in Gen. 1)
שׁקד	**139**	to be wakeful, watch (17)
אמל	**140**	to wither, decay, fade away (Pulal) (16)
בעת	**141**	to terrify (Pi., Ni.) (16)
דושׁ	**142**	to tread on, thresh (16)
חשׁה	**143**	to keep silence (16)
טבל	**144**	to dip into (16)
יצג	**145**	to set, place (Hi.) (16)
מור	**146**	to exchange, alter (Hi.) (16)
נשׁא (2) [3]	**147**	to beguile, deceive (Hi.) (16)
פרע	**148**	to loosen, neglect (16)
רגם (Qal)	**149**	to stone (16)
אזר (den.)	**150**	to put on, gird (15)

[1] For חפר (1), see p. 18, no. 63

[2] For נשׁא (2), see no. 147 below

[3] For נשׁא (1), see no. 133 above

אֵזוֹר	a.	loin-cloth (14, 8 in Jer. 13)
גזז	**151**	to shear, cut (15)
גער (Qal)	**152**	to rebuke (13)
גְּעָרָה	a.	rebuke (15)
גרה	**153**	to stir up (Pi.); to excite oneself (Hith.) (15)
דשׁן	**154**	to grow fat; to make fat (Pi.) (12)
דֶּשֶׁן	a.	fatness (15)
כבשׁ	**155**	to subdue (15)
נגן	**156**	to play a stringed instrument (Pi.) (15)
*נְגִינָה	a.	music of a stringed instrument; mocking song (14)
נשׁך (1)[1]	**157**	to bite (15)
עצב (2)[2]	**158**	to be grieved, downhearted (15)
פוח (1, 2) †	**159**	to breathe, blow against, launch forth, produce (15)
פצה (Qal)	**160**	to open the mouth (15)
צמת	**161**	to silence (15)
קדד (Qal)	**162**	to bow or kneel down (15)
קצר (2)[3]	**163**	to be short (15)
שׁרץ (Qal)	**164**	to swarm, teem (14)
שֶׁרֶץ	a.	swarming creatures (15)
ארג (Qal)	**165**	to weave (14)
בוז (Qal)	**166**	to despise (14)
בּוּז (f.), בּוּזָה	a.	contempt (12)
גדר (Qal)	**167**	to build a wall (10)
גָּדֵר, גֶּדֶר	a.	wall (of stones) (14)
*גְּדֵרָה	b.	(usually plu.) penfold of stones (9)
דמה (2)[4]	**168**	to be silent, cease (14)
דקק	**169**	to crush; to pulverize (Hi.) (13)
דַּק	a.	thin, scarce, fine (14)
חול	**170**	to dance round dances, turn upon (14)
מָחוֹל	a.	round dance (14)
מְחֹלָה (f.),		
חֵיל, חֵל	b.	rampart (9)
חכה (1) †	**171**	to wait for (Pi.) (14)

[1] For נשׁך (2), see p. 31, no. 174
[2] For עצב (1), see p. 29, no. 129
[3] For קצר (1), see p. 12, no. 34
[4] For דמה (1), see p. 14, no. 124

טול	**172**	to cast from afar, cast out (Hi.) (14)
כרה	**173**	to hollow, dig (14)
לוה (1)[1]	**174**	to join, accompany (Ni.) (14)
מחץ (Qal)	**175**	to break to pieces (14)
מרט	**176**	to polish; pluck (hair) (14)
סתם	**177**	to stop up, close (14)
עכר	**178**	to be taboo, cast out from social intercourse (14)
פגשׁ	**179**	to meet, encounter (14)
קבל	**180**	to receive, take (Pi.) (14)
קצץ (1)[2]	**181**	to cut off, to pieces (14)
שׁאף (Qal)	**182**	to gasp, pant after; snap at (14)
גזר (1) †	**183**	to cut in two, in pieces (13)
זיד (זוד)	**184**	to act presumptuously; to seethe, become heated or animated (Hi.) (10)
זֵד	a.	insolent, presumptuous (13)
זָדוֹן	b.	insolence, presumptuousness (11)
חבל (3)[3]	**185**	to act corruptly; to ruin (Pi.) (13)
חבק	**186**	to embrace (13)
חנף	**187**	to be polluted, apostate (11)
חָנֵף	a.	alienated from God, impious (13, 8 in Job)
טעם (Qal)	**188**	to taste (11)
טַעַם	a.	taste, discernment; decree (13)
עטף (2) †	**189**	to faint, languish (13)
ענה (4)[4]	**190**	to sing (13)
רעם (1) †	**191**	to thunder, storm (13)
שׁוט (1) †	**192**	to rove about (13)
שׁוֹט (1) †	a.	whip (11)
אנח	**193**	to sigh (Ni.) (12)
אֲנָחָה	a.	sigh, groan (10)
בוס	**194**	to tread down (12)
גאל (2)[5]	**195**	to be defiled, polluted (Ni., Pu.) (12)

[1] For לוה (2), see p. 21, no. 200
[2] For קצץ (2), see p. 27, no. 51
[3] For חבל (2), see p. 19, no. 116
[4] For ענה (1), see p. 5, no. 29;
ענה (2), see p. 9, no. 26;
ענה (3), see p. 25, no. 13
[5] For גאל (1), see p. 6, no. 8

גור (3)[1]	**196**	to be afraid of (12)
מָגוֹר	a.	horror (10)
מְגוֹרָה (f.),		
חפה	**197**	to cover (12)
† (1) חרץ	**198**	to decide, fix, determine (12)
טוח	**199**	to plaster, coat (12)
לוה (2)[2]	**200**	to borrow, lend (12)
נפח	**201**	to blow upon, breathe heavily, set aflame (12)
סעד (Qal)	**202**	to support, uphold, sustain (12)
עות	**203**	to make crooked, pervert (Pi.) (12)
שׁרק (Qal)	**204**	to whistle (12)
ארשׂ	**205**	to become engaged, betrothed (Pi.) (11)
דקר	**206**	to pierce through (11)
הדף (Qal)	**207**	to push, thrust (11)
† (1) חשׂף	**208**	to strip, lay bare (11)
חשק	**209**	to be attached to, love (11)
כנס	**210**	to gather (11)
להט	**211**	to devour, scorch, burn (11)
נבע	**212**	to bubble, flow (Hi.) (11)

[1] For גור (1), see p. 6, no. 10
[2] For לוה (1), see p. 20, no. 174

נחשׁ	**213**	to divine, look for omen (Pi.) (11)
נער (2)[1]	**214**	to shake (11)
צוק	**215**	to bring into straits, oppress, distress (Hi.) (11)
† (1) שׁבח	**216**	to praise, laud (Pi.); to boast (Hith.) (11)
שׁסה	**217**	to spoil, plunder (11)
שׁתל (Qal)	**218**	to transplant (11)
אוץ (Qal)	**219**	to urge, be in haste (10)
געל	**220**	to abhor, loathe (10)
געשׁ	**221**	to shake (10)
דחה	**222**	to push, cast or thrust down (10)
† (1) חרר	**223**	to be aglow; to be scorched (Ni.) (10)
נגח	**224**	to gore, push; to thrust at (Pi.) (10)
נגר	**225**	to run, flow, pour (Ni., Hi.) (10)
נהל	**226**	to lead (Pi.) (10)
ענג	**227**	to be of dainty habit, to take delight in (Hith.) (10)
פזר	**228**	to scatter, spread (10)
פרק	**229**	to tear off, rend (10)

[1] For נער (1), see p. 26, no. 23

LIST II

Verbal Roots
which Occur Less Than Ten Times,
With Their Nominal and Other Cognates
which Occur Ten or More Times

An Alphabetical Listing of Addenda to LIST II

אהל (2)† (den.) to pitch a tent
אֹהֶל (1)† a. tent

[Insert between Nos. 8d. and 9, p. 25.]

אנה (3)† to cause to occur, befall
(?) אֵת (2)† a. (prep.) with, beside (over 500)

[Insert between Nos. 1c. and 2, p. 25.]

זור (2)† to turn aside from, be estranged
זָר a. strange, different, illicit (70-99)

[Insert between Nos. 40a. and 41, p. 27.]

חלק (1)[1] to be smooth, slippery
חָלָק a. smooth (10)

[Insert between Nos. 183a. and 184, p. 31.]

חצצר (den.) to sound the trumpet
חֲצֹצְרָה a. trumpet, clarion (29, 16 in Chr.)

[Insert between Nos. 89b. and 90, p. 28.]

חרב (2)[2] (den.) to smite down, slaughter
חֶרֶב a. sword (300-500)

[Insert between Nos. 11c. and 12, p. 25.]

טפף (den.) (Qal) to trip along (Is. 3:16)
טַף a. little children (42)

[Insert between Nos. 69a. and 70, p. 28.]

[1] For חלק (2), see p. 10, No. 26.
[2] For חרב (1), see p. 13, No. 74.

כנף (den.) to hide oneself (Ni.) (Is. 30:20)
כָּנָף a. wing, skirt (of garment) (100-199)

[Insert between Nos. 30a. and 31, p. 26]

ספף (den.) to stand at the threshold (Hith.) (Ps. 84:11)
סַף a. threshold, sill (24)

[Insert between Nos. 104a. and 105, p. 29.]

עדר (3)† to be missed, lacking (Ni., Pi.)
עֵדֶר (1)† a. flock, herd (39)

[Insert between Nos. 71a. and 72, p. 28.]

(בְּנֵי) עַמּוֹן Ammon, Ammonites (106)

[Insert as No. 8c., p. 25.]

עפר (1)† (den.) to throw (earth) at (Pi.) (II Sa. 16:13)
עָפָר a. dry earth, dust (100-199)

[Insert between Nos. 33a. and 34, p. 26.]

פטר to escape from, set free
פֶּטֶר, *פִּטְרָה a. first-born (12)

[Insert between Nos. 170a. and 171, p. 31.]

II.

אדם	1	to be red, ruddy
אָדָם	a.	man, mankind (over 500)
אֲדָמָה	b.	ground (200-299)
אֱדוֹם	c.	Edom (70-99)
אשר (1)[1]	2	to walk straight; to lead on, reprove (Pi.)
אֲשֶׁר	a.	who, which, that (over 500)
אֲשֵׁרָה	b.	Asherah (goddess); sacred pole set up near altar (40)
אָשֻׁר*	c.	step (9)
כלל (Qal)	3	to perfect (the beauty of) (Ezek. 27 : 4, 11)
כֹּל	a.	all, every (over 500)
כָּלִיל	b.	entire, whole (15)
לבב (1) †	4	to cause the heart to beat (Cant. 4 : 9); to make intelligent (?) (Job 11 : 12) (Pi.)
לֵבָב, לֵב	a.	heart (over 500)
נפשׁ	5	to take breath, refresh oneself (Ni.)
נֶפֶשׁ	a.	throat; life, self (over 500)
עדה (1)[2]	6	to stride (Job 28 : 8); to remove (Prov. 25 : 20)
(?) עַד (2)[3]	a.	(prep.) Unto, as far as (spatial); until, while (temporal) (over 500)
עין (Qal) (den. of עַיִן)	7	to look suspiciously at (I Sa. 18:9, Ps. 49:6)
עַיִן	a.	eye, fountain (over 500)
מַעְיָן	b.	spring, fountain (23)
עמם (1) †	8	to ally oneself (Ps. 47 : 10); to come up to, be a match for (Ezek. 28 : 3, 31 : 8)
עַם	a.	people (over 500)
עִם	b.	(prep.) with (over 500)
עֻמָּה*	c.	close by, exactly as (32)
אלף (2) † (den. of אֶלֶף [2])	9	to produce in abundance, by thousands (Hi.) (Ps. 114 : 13)
אֶלֶף (2)	a.	thousand; tribe (300-500)
אַלּוּף (2) †	b.	chief, leader (63, 40 in Gen.)

אַלְפַּיִם	c.	two thousand (31)
אֶלֶף* (1)	d.	cattle (8)
אנשׁ	10	to be sickly, decrease (Ni.) (II Sa. 12 : 15)
אִשָּׁה	a.	woman (300-500)
אֱנוֹשׁ	b.	man, mankind (42)
חמשׁ (den. of חָמֵשׁ)	11	to be in battle array; to take the fifth part of (Pi.)
חָמֵשׁ, חֲמִשָּׁה	a.	five (300-500)
חֲמִשִּׁים	b.	fifty (100-199)
חֲמִישִׁי	c.	fifth (44)
כסף	12	to long for, be ashamed (?)
כֶּסֶף	a.	silver (300-500)
ענה (3)[1]	13	to be occupied, worried by
עַתָּה	a.	now (300-500)
עֵת	b.	time (300-500)
מַעַן, לְמַעַן	c.	(prep.) for the sake of, on account of; (conj.) in order that (100-199)
יַעַן	d.	(prep.) on account of; (conj.) because (70-99)
עקב (den. of עָקֵב)	14	to seize at the heel, beguile
יַעֲקֹב	a.	Jacob (300-500)
עָקֵב	b.	heel, footprints (14)
עֵקֶב (< עָקֵב)	c.	the hindmost, end; result, reward; (conj.) on account of, therefore (15)
עשׂר	15	to take or give a tenth of, tithe
עֶשֶׂר, עָשָׂר, עֲשָׂרָה, עֶשְׂרֵה,	a.	ten (300-500)
עֶשְׂרִים	b.	twenty (300-500)
מַעֲשֵׂר	c.	tenth part, tithe (31)
עִשָּׂרוֹן	d.	tenth part (30)
עֲשִׂירִי	e.	tenth (28)

[1] For אשר (2), see p. 28, no. 68
[2] For עדה (2), see p. 30, no. 155
[3] For עַד (1), see p. 38, no. 1

[1] For ענה (1), see p. 5, no. 29
ענה (2), see p. 9, no. 26
ענה (4), see p. 20, no. 190

עָשׂוֹר	f.	ten (16)
צהב (< זהב)	16	to gleam (Ho.) (Ez. 8 : 27)
זָהָב	a.	gold (300-500)
שׂרר	17	to rule, conduct
שַׂר	a.	official, leader (300-500)
שׁלשׁ (den. of שָׁלֹשׁ)	18	to divide in three parts, do or be at the third day, do for the third time. **(Pi.)**
שָׁלֹשׁ, שְׁלֹשָׁה	a.	three (300-500)
שְׁלִישִׁי	b.	third (100-199)
שְׁלֹשִׁים	c.	thirty (66)
שִׁלְשׁוֹם	d.	day before yesterday (25)
שָׁלִישׁ (3) †	e.	third man on a chariot; carrier of shield, adjutant (17)
ברה	19	to eat bread with, administer a patient's diet
בְּרִית	a.	covenant (200-299)
גבל (den.)	20	to set a boundary
גְּבוּל	a.	boundary, territory (200-299)
דבר (1) [1]	21	to turn aside, destroy, drive back
מִדְבָּר (1) †	a.	pasturage, wilderness, steppe (200-299)
דֶּבֶר (1) †	b.	plague (49)
חיל (2) [2]	22	to endure (Job 20 : 21; Ps. 10 : 5)
חַיִל	a.	strength, wealth, army (200-299)
נער (1) [3]	23	to growl (Jer. 51 : 38)
נַעַר (?)	a.	lad, youth (200-299)
נַעֲרָה	b.	young girl, maid (70-99)
נְעוּרִים	c.	early life, youth (46)
בדד (Qal)	24	to be isolated, alone
לְבַד	a.	alone (100-199)
בַּד (1) †	b.	part, portion (2 t.); linen (23 t.); stick, stave (43 t.)
בכר	25	to bear early, new fruit; to constitute as first-born (Pi.)
בְּכוֹר	a.	first-born (100-199)
בִּכּוּרִים	b.	first-fruits (17)
בְּכֹרָה	c.	right of first-born (15)
בקר	26	to attend to, bestow care on (Pi.)
בָּקָר	a.	cows, herd, cattle (100-199)

[1] For דבר (2), see p. 3, no. 4

[2] For חיל (1), see p. 13, no. 57

[3] For נער (2), see p. 21, no. 214

בֹּקֶר	b.	morning (100-199)
דור (Qal)	27	to stack in a circle (Ezek. 24 : 5); to circulate, dwell (Ps. 84 : 11)
דּוֹר	a.	generation, lifetime, life-span (100-
יחד	28	to be united
יַחַד	a.	together, at the same time (100-199)
יַחְדָּו	b.	together (70-99)
יָחִיד	c.	only one, alone, solitary (12)
ימן (den. of יָמִין)	29	to go to the right (Hi.)
יָמִין	a.	right hand or side; south (100-199)
יְמָנִי	b.	right hand, right (30)
תֵּימָן	c.	south (24)
יחם	30	to be hot; to be in breeding heat, conceive (Pi.)
חֵמָה	a.	heat, rage, wrath (100-199)
כפף	31	to bend, bow down
כַּף	a.	hand, palm (100-199)
לשׁן (den.)	32	to slander (Hi.) (Prov. 30 : 10; Ps. 101 : 5)
לָשׁוֹן	a.	tongue (100-199)
נהר (1) † (den.)	33	to stream
נָהָר	a.	stream, river (100-199)
ערב (4) [1] (den.)	34	to become evening
עֶרֶב	a.	evening (100-199)
מַעֲרָב (2) [2]	b.	sunset, west (14)
פעם	35	to impel, move, be disturbed
פַּעַם	a.	foot, step, time (100-199)
רעה (2) [3]	36	to have dealings with
רֵעַ	a.	fellow, companion, friend (100-199)
רַעְיָה*	b.	(female) companion, friend (10, 9 in Cant., 1 in Ju. 11 : 37)
שׁמן (den. of שֶׁמֶן)	37	to grow, be fat
שֶׁמֶן	a.	oil (100-199)
שָׁמֵן	b.	fat (10)
שׁקר	38	to deceive, deal falsely with (Pi.)
שֶׁקֶר	a.	lie, falsehood, deception (100-199)

[1] For ערב (1), see p. 18, no. 79

[2] For מַעֲרָב (1), see p. 18, no. 79a

[3] For רעה (1), see p. 7, no. 51

Hebrew	No.	English
אצר	**39**	to store up
אוֹצָר	a.	supply, store-house, treasure (70-99)
הבל (den.)	**40**	to be vain, empty
הֶבֶל (1) †	a.	breath, vanity, idol(s) (70-99, 37 in Ec.)
חלל (2) [1]	**41**	to pierce
חָלָל	a.	slain (70-99, 34 in Ezek.)
חַלּוֹן	b.	window (31)
חַלָּה	c.	ring-shaped bread (13)
חמר (2) †	**42**	to be reddened (Job 16 : 16)
חֲמוֹר (1) †	a.	male ass (70-99)
חֹמֶר (1)	b.	reddish-clay (17)
חֹמֶר (2)	c.	homer, dry measure; load of an ass (11)
כסל (Qal)	**43**	to be stupid (Jer. 10 : 8)
כְּסִיל	a.	insolent (religious); stupid, dull (in practical things) (70-90, 49 in Prov., 18 in Ec.)
כֶּסֶל (1, 2)	b.	loins; imperturbability, confidence (13)
לבן (1) [2]	**44**	to be or make white (Hi.)
לְבָנוֹן	a.	Lebanon (70-99)
לָבָן	b.	white (27, 18 in Lev. 13)
לְבֹנָה	c.	frankincense (20)
עור (2) [3]	**45**	to be naked (Ni.) (Hab. 3 : 9)
עוֹר	a.	skin, leather (70-99, 53 in Lev.)
קצה	**46**	to cut off, shorten (Pi.)
קָצֶה	a.	end, border, extremity (70-99)
קָצָה (*קְצָת)	b.	end, border, edge (33, 19 in Ex.)
קרן (den.)	**47**	to send out rays
קֶרֶן	a.	horn (70-99)
שאה (1) [4]	**48**	to be desolate, waste
שְׁאוֹל	a.	Sheol, underworld (69)
כרר	**49**	to dance, skip (II Sa. 6:14, 16)
כִּכָּר	a.	circuit; loaf; talent (68)
כַּר (1) †	b.	ram (13)
עמק	**50**	to make deep

[1] For חלל (1), see p. 6, no. 17
[2] For לבן (2), see p. 31, no. 166
[3] For עור (1), see p. 29, no. 96
עור (3), see p. 9, no. 24
[4] For שאה (2), see p. 30, no. 136

Hebrew	No.	English
עֵמֶק	a.	vale, plain (68)
עָמֹק	b.	deep (18)
קצץ (2) [1] (den.)	**51**	to come to an end (Hi.) (Ps. 55 : 24, 138 : 18)
קֵץ	a.	end (66)
גנן (Qal)	**52**	to enclose, fence, defend
מָגֵן (1) †	a.	shield (63)
גַּן, גַּנָּה (f.)	b.	garden (57)
שמאל (den.)	**53**	to go to the left (Hi.)
שְׂמֹאול	a.	left (side), north (63)
אצל	**54**	to set aside, take away, reduce
אֵצֶל	a.	(prep.) beside (61)
חמס	**55**	to treat violently
חָמָס	a.	violence, wrong, lawlessness (60)
שׂער (1) †	**56**	to bristle
שָׂעִיר	a.	hairy; male goat, buck (59, 27 in Num., 23 in Lev.)
שֵׂעָר	b.	hair (36)
שְׂעֹרָה	c.	barley (33)
ארח (Qal)	**57**	to be on the road, wander
אֹרַח	a.	road, path, way (58)
פרשׁ	**58**	to declare distinctly, explain
פָּרָשׁ	a.	horseman (57)
קטן	**59**	to be insignificant, small
קָטֹן	a.	small (54)
קָטָן	b.	small (46)
ירע (Qal)	**60**	to quiver (Isa. 15 : 4)
יְרִיעָה	a.	tent curtain (53, 43 in Ex.)
שׁוא	**61**	to treat badly (Hi.)
שָׁוְא	a.	in vain, worthless (52)
שׁוֹאָה	b.	trouble, storm (13)
שׁנן (1) †	**62**	to sharpen
שֵׁן	a.	tooth (52)
אפד (Qal)	**63**	to make the dress close fitting (Ex. 29 : 5; Lev. 8 : 7)
אֵפוֹד	a.	ephod (50, 29 in Ex.)
צלל (3) [2]	**64**	to be shadowy, dark (Neh. 13 : 19; Ezek. 31 : 3)
צֵל	a.	shadow (49)
גאה (Qal)	**65**	to be high, exalted
גָּאוֹן	a.	height; pride (49)

[1] For קצץ (1), see p. 20, no. 181
[2] For צלל (1), see p. 30, no. 161

גַּאֲוָה	b.	haughtiness (19)
גֵּאֶה	c.	haughty (10)
פסח	66	to be lame, limp
פֶּסַח	a.	Passover (49)
פִּסֵּחַ	b.	lame (14)
דלל (Qal)	67	to be little, low
דַּל (2) †	a.	low, helpless, poor (46)
אשר (2) [1] (den.)	68	to pronounce happy, call blessed (Pi.)
אֶשֶׁר*	a.	introductory word of blessing: blessed, happy (44, 26 in Ps.)
אפס (Qal)	69	to come to an end, cease
אֶפֶס	a.	end; nothing, non-existence; notwithstanding, howbeit (42)
יפה	70	to be beautiful
יָפֶה	a.	fair, beautiful (40)
יְפִי*	b.	beauty (18)
עלל (2) [2]	71	to insert, thrust in (Job 16 : 15)
עֹל	a.	yoke (40)
חדר (Qal)	72	to surround (Ezek. 21 : 19)
חֶדֶר	a.	dark room, chamber (38)
מלל (3) †	73	to say, utter (Pi.)
מִלָּה	a.	word (38, 34 in Job)
אבל (2) [3]	74	to dry up
תֵּבֵל	a.	world, continent (36)
חסד (2) † (den. of חָסִיד)	75	to act as pious (one) (Hith.) (II Sa. 22 : 26; Ps. 18 : 26)
חֶסֶד (1) †	a.	loyalty, devotion, steadfast love (200-299)
חָסִיד	b.	loyal, pious one (35, 26 in Ps.)
גשם	76	to send rain (Jer. 14 : 22; Ezek. 22 : 24)
גֶּשֶׁם	a.	rain (34)
עבר (2) [4]	77	to show oneself infuriated (Hith.)
עֶבְרָה	a.	anger, fury (34)
ערל (den. of עָרְלָה)	78	to leave uncircumcised (Lev. 19 : 23; Hab. 2 : 16)
עָרֵל	a.	uncircumcised; unskilled to speak (34, 15 in Ezek.)
עָרְלָה	b.	foreskin (16)

[1] For אשר (1), see p. 25, no. 2
[2] For עלל (1), see p. 17, no. 31
[3] For אבל (1), see p. 13, no. 84
[4] For עבר (1), see p. 3, no. 16

אלה (1) †	79	to swear, curse
אָלָה	a.	curse (33)
גדד	80	to gather together against; to administer incisions to oneself
גְּדוּד (2) †	a.	band, troop; raid (33)
שרש (den.)	81	to root out, take root
שֹׁרֶשׁ	a.	root (33)
נוה (1) † (#)	82	to reach one's aim (Hab. 2 : 5)
נָוֶה (#)	a.	pasture-ground; abode (32)
רמה (1) [1]	83	to throw, shoot
אַרְמוֹן	a.	fortified dwelling-tower (32)
עוב	84	to becloud (Hi.) (Lam. 2 : 1)
עָב (2) †	a.	clouds (31)
פסל (Qal)	85	to cut, hew stones
פֶּסֶל	a.	idol (31)
פְּסִיל*	b.	(only plur.) idol (23)
הדר	86	to honor, prefer
הָדָר	a.	ornament, splendor, majesty (30)
חנט (Qal)	87	to gain the color of ripeness (Cant. 2 : 13); to embalm (Gen. 50 : 2, 26)
חִטָּה	a.	wheat (30)
נדה (1) †	88	to exclude (Is. 66 : 5); to refuse to think of (Pi.) (Am. 6 : 3)
נִדָּה	a.	excretion; abhorrent thing; impurity, menstruation (30)
עול (1) [2]	89	to act wrongfully (Pi.) (Is. 26 : 10; Ps. 71 : 4)
עַוְלָה	a.	unrighteousness, wickedness (30)
עָוֶל	b.	injustice, unrighteousness (21)
ברד (1) †	90	to hail (Is. 32 : 19)
בָּרָד	a.	hail (28, 17 in Ex.)
רכש (Qal)	91	to gather property (Gen.)
רְכוּשׁ	a.	property, goods (28)
שרד (Qal)	92	to run away (Josh. 10 : 20)
שָׂרִיד (1) †	a.	survivor (28)
שקץ	93	to detest as unclean (Pi.)
שִׁקּוּץ	a.	heathen detested idol, detested thing (28)
שֶׁקֶץ	b.	detestable thing (11, 9 in Lev.)
אדר	94	to be mighty, powerful, glorious
אַדִּיר	a.	mighty (26)

[1] For רמה (2), see p. 17, no. 33
[2] For עול (2), see p. 29, no. 117

אַדֶּרֶת	b.	splendor; state robe or coat (12)
הון	**95**	to regard as easy (Hi.) (Deut. 1 : 41)
הוֹן	a.	wealth, power (26, 18 in Prov.)
עור (1) [1]	**96**	to make blind(Pi.)
עִוֵּר	a.	blind (26)
שׂטן (Qal)	**97**	to bear a grudge, cherish animosity
שָׂטָן	a.	adversary (26, 14 in Job 1-2)
ברך (1) [2] (den.)	**98**	to kneel, bow down
בֶּרֶךְ	a.	knee (25)
עשׁן (Qal)	**99**	to smoke
עָשָׁן	a.	(ascending) smoke (25)
פחח (den.)	**100**	to be entrapped, ensnared (Hi.) (Is. 42 : 22)
פַּח	a.	bird-trap, snare (25)
שׁטר*	**101**	to write (occurs only in ptc. below)
שֹׁטֵר	a.	scribe; officer (25)
כתר	**102**	to surround
כֹּתֶרֶת*	a.	capital of pillar (24, 16 in I Kgs.)
נשׁם (Qal)	**103**	to pant (Is. 42 : 14)
נְשָׁמָה	a.	breath (24)
סער	**104**	to grow stormy
סַעַר	a.	tempest (24)
סְעָרָה (f.)		
דמע (Qal)	**105**	to shed tears (Jer. 13 : 17)
דִּמְעָה	a.	tears (23)
עטר	**106**	to surround; crown a person
עֲטָרָה	a.	crown, wreath (23)
צהר	**107**	to press out oil (?) (Hi.) (Job 24 : 11)
יִצְהָר	a.	oil (23)
צָהֳרַיִם	b.	midday, noon (23)
שׁוח (den.)	**108**	to run down (Prov. 2 : 18)
שַׁחַת	a.	pit, grave (23)
שׁחד (Qal)	**109**	to give a present (Ezek. 16 : 33; Job 6 : 22)
שֹׁחַד	a.	present, bribe (23)
חתה (2) †	**110**	to rake together
מַחְתָּה	a.	fire-holder (22)
נעל	**111**	to lock, bar

[1] For עור (2), see p. 27, no. 45;
עור (3), see p. 9, no. 24
[2] For ברך (2), see p. 4, no. 6

נַעַל	a.	sandal (22)
פגר	**112**	to be (too) faint, tired (Pi.) (I Sa. 30 : 10, 21)
פֶּגֶר	a.	corpse (22)
צער (Qal)	**113**	to be insignificant
צָעִיר	a.	little, small, young (22)
רגע	**114**	to come to rest, repose
רֶגַע	a.	moment (22)
ברק (Qal)	**115**	to light, illumine
בָּרָק (1) †	a.	lightning (21)
נסס	**116**	to falter; run zigzag; to glitter
נֵס	a.	standard, signal, sign (21)
עול (2) [1]	**117**	to give suck
עוֹלָל, עוֹלֵל	a.	child (21)
שׁחק (Qal)	**118**	to rub away, pulverize
שַׁחַק	a.	dust, clouds (21)
נגה	**119**	to shine
נֹגַהּ	a.	brightness (20)
קלט (Qal)	**120**	to be stunted, shortened (Lev. 22 : 23)
מִקְלָט	a.	refuge, asylum (20)
שׁלג (den.)	**121**	to snow (Hi.) (Ps. 68 : 15)
שֶׁלֶג (1) †	a.	snow (20)
חמץ (1) †	**122**	to be leavened
חָמֵץ	a.	leaven, what is leavened (19)
רען	**123**	to grow luxuriant (Job 15 : 32)
רַעֲנָן	a.	luxuriant, full of leaves (19)
שׂיב (Qal)	**124**	to be gray, old (I Sa. 12 : 2; Job 15 : 10)
שֵׂיבָה	a.	gray-headed; old age (19)
שׁגג (Qal)	**125**	to commit error, sin inadvertently
שְׁגָגָה	a.	sin of error, inadvertence (19)
שׁוק	**126**	to prove (too) narrow, overflow
שׁוֹק	a.	thigh (19)
אפק	**127**	to contain, control oneself (Hith.)
אָפִיק	a.	channel, stream-bed (18)
הוה (1) †	**128**	to fall (Job 37 : 6)
הַוָּה*	a.	destruction (18)
עצב (1) [2]	**129**	to intertwine, shape (Job 10 : 8); to make an image (Jer. 44 : 19)
עָצָב*	a.	(only plu.) idol, image (18)

[1] For עול (1), see p. 28, no. 89
[2] For עצב (2), see p. 20, no. 158

קוּר (Qal)	**130**	to dig (for water) (II Kgs. 19 : 24; Is. 37 : 25)
מָקוֹר	a.	well (18)
קין	**131**	to chant a lament (Polel)
† (1) קִינָה	a.	elegy, dirge (18, 10 in Ezek.)
חפשׁ	**132**	to free (Lev. 19 : 20)
חָפְשִׁי	a.	released, emancipated from slavery (17)
† (2) עיף	**133**	to be faint
עָיֵף	a.	weary, faint (17)
† (2) קלה	**134**	to be lightly esteemed, treat with contempt
קָלוֹן	a.	ignominy, dishonor (17)
רכל*	**135**	to trade (occurs only in ptc. below)
רֹכֵל	a.	trader (17, 11 in Ezek.)
שׁאה (2)[1]	**136**	to roar (Ni.) (Is. 17 : 12-13)
† (2) שָׁאוֹן	a.	roar, din (17)
תפף (den.)	**137**	to beat the timbrel
תֹּף	a.	timbrel, tambourine (17)
זול (Qal)	**138**	to lavish gold (Is. 46 : 6)
זוּלָה*	a.	except, only (16)
כאב	**139**	to be in pain; mar (Hi.)
מַכְאוֹב	a.	pain (16)
† (1) נטר	**140**	to keep, guard (Cant. 1 : 6, 8 : 11)
מַטָּרָה	a.	target; guard (16, 11 in Jer.)
סוף	**141**	to come to an end
סוּפָה	a.	storm-wind (16)
סמם	**142**	to cover with paste, perfume, paint one's face, color (Hi.) (II Kgs. 9 : 30; Job 13 : 27)
סַם*	a.	(only plu.) paste, perfume (16, 11 in Ex.)
† (2) קלע	**143**	to carve (I Kgs. 6 : 29, 32 : 35)
† (2) קֶלַע*	a.	curtain (16, 13 in Ex.)
קשׁשׁ	**144**	to gather, collect
קַשׁ	a.	stubble (16)
רכך	**145**	to be soft, timid
רַךְ	a.	tender, delicate, weak (16)
מתח (Qal)	**146**	to spread out (Is. 40 : 22)
אַמְתַּחַת	a.	sack (15, Gen.)
עוז	**147**	to take refuge
עֹז (2)[2]	a.	protection, refuge (15)

[1] For שׁאה (1), see p. 27, no. 48

[2] For עֹז (1), see p. 16, 21a

† (1) צוץ	**148**	to blossom
צִיץ, צִיצָה (f.)	a.	blossom; front ornament (15)
צמד	**149**	to put to, attach to
צֶמֶד	a.	couple, span (15)
תאר	**150**	to turn, incline; trace, outline
תֹּאַר	a.	form (15)
דגל (den.)	**151**	to lift a banner
דֶּגֶל	a.	banner; division of a tribe (14, 13 in Num., 1 in Cant. 2 : 4)
דשׁא	**152**	to grow green (Gen. 1 : 11; Jo. 2 : 22)
דֶּשֶׁא	a.	new grass (14)
יגה	**153**	to vex, grieve, be depressed
יָגוֹן	a.	grief, vexation (14)
† (2) מלח (den.)	**154**	to salt
† (2) מֶלַח	a.	salt (14)
עדה (2)[1]	**155**	to deck oneself with ornaments
עֲדִי	a.	ornaments (14)
עצל	**156**	to be sluggish (Ni.) (Ju. 18 : 19)
עָצֵל	a.	sluggish, lazy (14, Prov.)
פתת (Qal)	**157**	to crumble (Lev. 2 : 6)
פַּת	a.	bit, morsel (14)
צעד	**158**	to step, march
צַעַד*	a.	marching, pace, step (14)
ברא (2)[2]	**159**	to make fat (Hi.) (I Sa. 2 : 29)
בָּרִיא	a.	fat (13)
צחח (Qal)	**160**	to be white (Lam. 4 : 7)
מֵצַח (?)	a.	forehead (13)
צלל (1)[3]	**161**	to tingle
מְצִלְתַּיִם	a.	cymbals (13, 11 in Chr.)
צנף (Qal)	**162**	to wrap (Is. 22 : 18); to wind (Lev. 16 : 4)
מִצְנֶפֶת	a.	turban (13, 9 in Ex.)
קנן	**163**	to nest, make a nest (Pi.)
קֵן	a.	nest (13)
דבב (Qal)	**164**	to flow over softly (Cant. 7 : 10)
דֹּב	a.	bear (12)
דִּבָּה	b.	whispering, evil report (9)

[1] For עדה (1), see p. 25, no. 6

[2] For ברא (1), see p. 10, no. 39

[3] For צלל (3), see p. 27, no. 64

הום	**165**	to be in a stir, throw in disorder
מְהוּמָה	a.	confusion, consternation (12)
לבן (2)[1]	**166**	to make brick (Gen. 11 : 3; Ex. 5 : 7, 14)
לְבֵנָה	a.	sun-baked brick, tile (12, 7 in Ex.)
נעם (Qal)	**167**	to be pleasant
נָעִים	a.	pleasant, delightful (12)
נשף (Qal)	**168**	to blow (Ex. 15 : 10); blow upon (Is. 40 : 24)
נֶשֶׁף	a.	morning (or evening) darkness (12)
נתח	**169**	to cut in pieces (Pi.)
נֵתַח	a.	piece of meat (12)
עקר	**170**	to root up, weed cut; to hamstring (Pi.)
עָקָר	a.	barren, without offspring (12)
עֲקָרָה (f.),		
קוץ (1) †	**171**	to feel a loathing at
קוֹץ	a.	thorn-bush (12)
רקם	**172**	to variegate, weave in colors (Ex.)
רִקְמָה	a.	variegated stuff (12, 8 in Ex.)
זכך	**173**	to be pure, clean, bright
זַךְ	a.	pure (11)
נשך (2)[2] (den.)	**174**	to claim interest
נֶשֶׁךְ	a.	interest (money) (11)
עקשׁ	**175**	to pervert, defraud, be guilty, crooked
עִקֵּשׁ	a.	crooked, perverted (11, 7 in Prov.)
ערם (2)[3]	**176**	to be crafty, cunning
עָרוּם	a.	shrewd (11, 8 in Prov.)
פתח (2)[4]	**177**	to engrave (Pi.)
פִּתּוּחַ	a.	engraving (11)
פתל	**178**	to twist, prove tortuous, astute

[1] For לבן (1), see p. 27, no. 44
[2] For נשך (1), see p. 20, no. 157
[3] For ערם (1), see no. 188 below
[4] For פתח (1), see p. 7, no. 42

פְּתִיל	a.	twisted thread, cord (11)
קצע (2) †	**179**	to make with a corner structure
מִקְצוֹעַ	a.	corner-post (11)
קרח (1) †	**180**	to make bald
קָרְחָה	a.	baldness (11)
בדק (Qal)	**181**	to mend, repair
בֶּדֶק	a.	breach (10, 8 in II Kgs.)
בלה (<בהל)	**182**	to dishearten (Pi.) (Ez. 4 : 4)
בַּלָּהָה	a.	sudden terror (10)
זנב (den.)	**183**	to cut off, smite the tail (Pi.) (Deut. 25 : 18, Josh. 10 : 19)
זָנָב	a.	tail, end, stump (10)
כבר	**184**	to multiply words (Hi.) (Job 35 : 16, 36 : 31)
כַּבִּיר	a.	great, mighty (10)
מתק	**185**	to be sweet
מָתוֹק	a.	sweet (10)
נשק (2)[1]	**186**	to be equipped with (I Chr. 12 : 2; II Chr. 17 : 17)
נֶשֶׁק	a.	equipment, armory (10)
עמר (2) †	**187**	to deal violently with (Hith.) (Deut. 21 : 14, 24 : 7)
עֹמֶר (2) †	a.	omer (measure of grain) (10, Ex. 16, Lev. 23)
ערם (1)[2]	**188**	to heap up, be gathered, dammed up (Ex. 15 : 8)
עֲרֵמָה	a.	heap (10)
פלג	**189**	to divide (Gen. 10 : 25; I Chr. 1 : 19); to cleave (Job 38 : 25)
פֶּלֶג (1) †	a.	artificial channel, canal (10)
קרס (Qal)	**190**	to bend down, stoop (Is. 46 : 1-2)
קֶרֶס*	a.	(only plu.) hook (10, Ex.)
שׁאן	**191**	to be at ease, secure
שַׁאֲנָן	a.	at ease, secure (10)
שׁפה	**192**	to sweep bare (Is. 13 : 2); to be without flesh (Job 33 : 11)
שְׁפִי	a.	bare hill; piste, track (10)

[1] For נשק (1), see p. 14, no. 123
[2] For ערם (2), see no. 176 above

LIST III

Nouns and Other Words
Without Extant Verbal Cognates
in the Hebrew Bible

An Alphabetical Listing of Addenda to LIST III

אִי (1)† coast, island (36)

[Insert between Nos. 37 and 38, p. 38.]

אַיָּלָה doe (10)

[Insert as No. 103a., p. 41.]

אֵילָם* porch (of temple) (16, Ezek. 40)

[Insert between Nos. 53 and 54, p. 40.]

אֵיפֹה(א), אֵפוֹא where?; then, so (25)

[Insert between Nos. 83 and 84, p. 39.]

אֵלוֹן (1)† large tree (10)

[Insert between Nos. 116 and 117, p. 41.]

אָנָּא(ה) I(we) pray(beseech) you (13)

[Insert as III B. 10a., p. 35.]

אֵשׁ[1] fire

[Insert between Nos. 1 and 2 in list III B., p. 35.]

אַתְּ, אַתֵּן you (fem.s. and plu.) (50-69)

[Insert as No. 13a. in List III A., p. 35.]

זוּ this, who (14)

[Insert as No. 20a., p. 35.]

[1] Cf. with III F. 2, p. 37.

יְרִיחוֹ Jericho (57, 29 in Josh.)

[Insert as No. 78a., p. 39.]

כִּי־אִם unless, except, but

[Insert as No. 24a., p. 35.]

כָּכָה thus (34)

[Insert as No. 23a., p. 35.]

כְּמוֹ as, like

[Insert between Nos. 11 and 12 in List III D. p. 36.]

לוּ, לֻא O that, would that, if only (22)

[Insert as No. 25b., p. 35.]

מְצוֹלָה, מְצֻלָה depth, abyss (12)

[Insert between Nos. 98 and 99, p 41.]

עַשְׁתֵּי one (but used only with עָשָׂר, עֶשְׂרֵה to mean "eleven, eleventh") (19)

[Insert between Nos. 32 and 33, p. 40.]

קֶרֶשׁ board (49, 45 in Ex.)

[Insert between Nos. 1a. and 2, p. 38.]

שִׁמְשׁוֹן Samson (38, Ju.)

[Insert as No. 30a. in List III D., p. 37.]

III A. Words Occurring Over 500 Times

אָב	1	father
אָדוֹן, אֲדֹנָי	2	lord, master, the Lord
אָח	3	brother
אֶחָד	4	one
אַיִן (1)[1]	5	non-existence; as quasi-verb: there is not . . .
אִישׁ	6	man
אֶל	7	(prep.) unto, toward
אַל	8	no, not (often used for temporary negation; also negative of imp. and juss.)
אֱלֹהִים	9	God
אֵל	a.	God (200-299)
אֱלוֹהַּ	b.	God (58, 41 in Job)
אִם	10	(conj.) if, when
אָנֹכִי, אֲנִי	11	I
אֶרֶץ	12	earth
אַתָּה, אַתֶּם (m., s. and plu.)	13	you
בַּיִת, בֵּית (cstr.)	14	house
גַּם	15	also
הוּא	16	he
הִיא	17	she
הֵם, הֵמָּה (m.)	18	they
הַר	19	mountain
זֶה, זֹאת (f.)	20	this

[1] For אַיִן* (2), see p. 40, no. 34

אֵלֶּה (plu. c.)		these
יָד	21	hand
יוֹם	22	day
יוֹמָם	a.	daily (51)
כֹּה	23	thus, so
כִּי	24	because, for, that, when, but
לֹא	25	no, not (often used for permanent negation)
אוּלַי	a.	perhaps (43)
לוּלֵי, לוּלֵא	b.	if not, unless (13)
מֵאָה	26	hundred
מָאתַיִם	a.	two hundred (70-99)
מָה	27	what? how?
בַּמֶּה	a.	wherewith?
כַּמָּה	b.	how much? how many? how long?
לָמָּה	c.	why?
מֵי*, מַיִם	28	water
עִיר	29	city
קוֹל	30	voice, sound
רֹאשׁ (1)[1]	31	head
רִאשׁוֹן	a.	first (100-199)
רֵאשִׁית	b.	first, beginning (51)
מְרַאֲשׁוֹת*	c.	place at the head (10)
שֵׁם	32	name
שָׁם	33	there

[1] For רֹאשׁ (2), see p. 41, no. 100

III B. Words Occurring 300-500 Times

אֹהֶל (#)	1	tent
בְּהֵמָה (#)	2	cattle, animals
גּוֹי (#)	3	people, nation
דָּם	4	blood
הִנֵּה	5	behold, lo
חֶרֶב (#)	6	sword
יָם	7	sea
כְּלִי	8	vessel, utensil
מִי	9	who
נָא	10	particle of entreaty: pray, now; please

נְאֻם	11	utterance
עוֹלָם	12	remote time (past or future); forever
עֵץ	13	tree (also collective)
פֶּה	14	mouth
לְפִי, כְּפִי	a.	(conj.) according to
שָׂדַי, שָׂדֶה	15	open field
שָׁמַיִם	16	heavens
† (1) שַׁעַר	17	gate
שׁוֹעֵר	a.	gate-keeper (37, 20 in Chr.)
תָּוֶךְ	18	midst
תּוֹךְ (cstr.),		
תִּיכוֹן	a.	middle (12)
תַּחַת	19	(prep.) under
תַּחְתּוֹן, תַּחְתִּי	a.	the lower, lowest (29)

III C. Words Occurring 200-299 Times

אֶבֶן	1	stone
אוֹ	2	(conj.) or
[1] (1) אַיִל	3	ram
אֵם	4	mother
† (1) אַמָּה	5	forearm, cubit
אָרוֹן	6	ark
בָּשָׂר	7	flesh
(לַיִל) לַיְלָה	8	night
מְאֹד	9	force might; adv.: very, exceedingly

[1] For אַיִל (3), see p. 39, no. 16

[1] מַלְאָךְ		
(< לאךְ*)	10	messenger
מִנְחָה	11	gift, offering
מִשְׁפָּחָה	12	family, clan
[2] (1) שֵׁשׁ	13	six
שִׁשִּׁים	a.	sixty (58)
שִׁשִּׁי	b.	sixth (27)

[1] Cf. with III D, 19 below

[2] For שֵׁשׁ (3), see p. 38, no. 31

III D. Words Occurring 100-199 Times

אָז	1	then
מֵאָז	a.	formerly, since
אָחוֹת	2	sister
אַךְ	3	only, surely
אֲנַחְנוּ	4	we
[1] (1) אַף	5	also, even, the more so
בָּמָה	6	high place, funerary installation
בַּעַד	7	distance; (prep.) behind, through, round about, for (the benefit of)
[2] הֵן	8	behold; if
חוֹמָה	9	wall
חוּץ	10	place outside the house, street; (prep.) outside, without
חִיצוֹן	a.	outer, external (24, 17 in Ezek.)

[1] For אַף (2), see p. 16, no. 7a

[2] Cf. with III B. 5 above, p. 35

חָצֵר	11	permanent settlement, court, enclosure
יַיִן	12	wine
יֵשׁ	13	there is (quasi-verb)
כֶּבֶשׂ,		
also כֶּשֶׂב	14	young ram (both with same meaning)
כֹּחַ	15	strength, power
(#)כָּנָף	16	wing
כִּסֵּא	17	seat, throne
(#)כֶּרֶם	18	vineyard
(#) כַּרְמֶל	a.	orchard (16)
[1] מְלָאכָה	19	work
(> לאךְ*)		
נֶגֶב	20	the dry country, south, Negeb

[1] Cf. with III C. 10 above

נַחַל	**21**	torrent valley, wadi
נְחֹשֶׁת	**22**	copper, bronze
נְחוּשָׁה	a.	bronze (10)
סוּס	**23**	horse
(#)עָפָר	**24**	dust
פַּר	**25**	young bull
פָּרָה	a.	cow (26)
† (2) רַק	**26**	only
שָׂפָה	**27**	lip
שֵׁבֶט	**28**	rod, staff, tribe
שְׁמֹנֶה	**29**	eight
שְׁמֹנִים	a.	eighty (38)
שְׁמִינִי	b.	eighth (30)
שֶׁמֶשׁ	**30**	sun
תָּמִיד	**31**	continually; regular

III E. Words Occurring 70-99 Times

אָוֶן	**1**	wickedness, iniquity
אוֹת	**2**	sign
אֶרֶז	**3**	cedar
אֲרִי, (f.) אַרְיֵה	**4**	lion
בֶּטֶן	**5**	belly, womb
בַּרְזֶל	**6**	iron
בְּתוּלָה	**7**	virgin
בְּתוּלִים	a.	stage of virginity (10)
גּוֹרָל	**8**	lot
דֶּלֶת	**9**	door
הֵיכָל	**10**	palace, temple
זָכָר	**11**	male
זְרוֹעַ	**12**	arm, forearm
חֵלֶב	**13**	fat (47 in Lev.)
כְּרוּב	**14**	cherub (32 in Ezek.)
סֶלָה	**15**	selah (unexplained technical term of music or recitation) (71 in Ps.)
† (1) פֵּאָה	**16**	side, rim, corner (47 in Ezek.)
† (1) צוּר	**17**	rock
קִיר	**18**	wall
קֶשֶׁת	**19**	bow
שׁוֹפָר	**20**	ram's horn, trumpet
שׁוֹר	**21**	bullock, steer
שֻׁלְחָן	**22**	table

III F. Words Occurring 69-50 Times

כָּתֵף	**1**	shoulder; slope, side of mountain (67)
אִשֶּׁה	**2**	fire-offering (66, 42 in Lev.)
בּוֹר	**3**	cistern, pit (66)
שִׁפְחָה	**4**	maidservant (63, 28 in Gen.)
יְאוֹר, יְאֹר	**5**	River Nile; stream, river (63, 26 in Ex.)
יָרֵךְ	**6**	upper thigh, hip (62)
(f.) *יְרֵכָה	a.	backside, remotest part, innermost part (28)
סֶלַע	**7**	crag, cliff, rock (62)
אֵיךְ	**8**	how? (60)
אֵיכָה	a.	how? where? (21)
גִּבְעָה	**9**	hill (60)
† (2) עֲרָבָה	**10**	desert (60)
† (1) יַעַר	**11**	thicket, woodland, forest (59)
דּוֹד	**12**	beloved one; uncle, cousin; love (59, 36 in Cant.)
חֵץ	**13**	arrow (58)
תֵּשַׁע	**14**	nine (58)
תִּשְׁעִים	a.	ninety (19)
תְּשִׁיעִי	b.	ninth (17)
אֶדֶן	**15**	pedestal, socket (57, 51 in Ex.)
אַלְמָנָה	**16**	widow (56)
אָמָה	**17**	handmaid (56)
גֶּפֶן	**18**	vine (55)
טֶרֶם	**19**	(conj.) before (55)
גָּמָל	**20**	camel (54, 25 in Gen.)
דְּבַשׁ	**21**	honey (54)

פֹּה 22 here, hither (54)

סֹלֶת 23 wheat, groats (53, 34 in Lev.-Num.)

† (1) חֶבֶל 24 cord, rope (51)

קָנֶה 25 reed, shaft, stalk (61)

III G. Words Occurring 49-25 Times

עַד (1)[1] 1 forever (49)

לָעַד a. forever (21)

תְּכֵלֶת 2 violet-purple dye or wool (49, 34 in Ex.)

מַצָּה 3 unleavened bread (48)

שַׂק 4 loin covering of mourning; sackcloth (48)

שַׁדַּי 5 Shaddai (48, 31 in Job)

הוֹי 6 (int.) ah! alas! (47, 21 in Is.)

חֲנִית 7 spear (47, 30 in Sa.)

לִשְׁכָּה 8 room, hall (47, 23 in Ezek.)

מָתְנַיִם 9 loins (47)

אַיֵּה, אַי 10 where? (45)

חָלָב 11 milk (45)

נֵר 12 lamp (44)

מְנוֹרָה a. lampstand (39, 19 in Ex.)

שֶׂה 13 lamb or goat kid (44)

יָתוֹם 14 fatherless, orphan (42)

טַף(#) 15 little children (42)

לוּחַ 16 (stone) tablet (42)

מְעָרָה 17 cave (42)

† (1) שָׁנִי 18 scarlet (42, 26 in Ex.)

מָתַי 19 when? (42)

עַד־מָתַי a. how long?

סָרִיס 20 court official, eunuch (42)

† (1) הֵנָּה 21 hither (41)

כִּנּוֹר 22 zither (41)

צַוָּאר 23 neck (41)

דָּגָן 24 corn, grain (40)

צִפּוֹר 25 bird (40)

דַּי 26 sufficiency, enough (39)

מִדֵּי a. (conj.) as often as

תְּאֵנָה 27 fig tree (39)

אֳנִי, אֳנִיָּה 28 ship(s); fleet (38)

זַיִת 29 olive tree (38)

חֵיק 30 bosom (38)

שֵׁשׁ (3)[1] 31 (Egyptian) linen (38, 32 in Ex.)

תּוֹלֵעָה, תּוֹלַעַת 32 maggot, worm; crimson cloth (38, 26 in Ex.)

אַרְגָּמָן 33 wool dyed with red purple (37, 25 in Ex.)

† (1) בְּאֵר 34 water-place, well, pit (37)

מוּל, מוֹל 35 forefront; (prep.) in front of (37)

פִּילֶגֶשׁ, פִּלֶגֶשׁ 36 concubine (37)

צֵלָע 37 side; side-chambers, wing (37, 17 in Ex.)

כּוֹכָב 38 star (36)

מוֹפֵת 39 sign, token (36)

אֵיפָה 40 ephah (corn measure) (35)

לְאֹם 41 people, nation (35)

עֵגֶל 42 young bull (35)

עֲגָלָה a. cart, chariot (25)

עֶגְלָה b. cow (14)

† (2) מַעְגָּל c. track (of wagon) ; course (13, 7 in Prov.)

תְּהוֹם 43 primeval ocean, deep (35)

דָּג, דָּגָה (f.) 44 fish (34)

כַּלָּה 45 bride, daughter-in-law (34)

עֹרֶף 46 neck (33)

עֵשֶׂב 47 herb, herbage (33)

אוֹפָן 48 wheel (32, 23 in Ezek.)

גֹּרֶן 49 threshing-floor (32)

יוֹנָה 50 dove (32)

כֶּלֶב 51 dog (32)

מְאוּמָה 52 something (32)

מְאוּם, מאוּם, מוּם a. blemish, defect (22)

[1] For עַד (2), see p. 25, no. 6a

[1] For שֵׁשׁ (1), see p. 36, III C. no. 13

*מֵעִים	**53**	bowels, belly, inward parts (32)
נֹכַח	**54**	(prep.) in front of, over against (32)
אֶצְבַּע	**55**	finger (31)
גָּג	**56**	roof (31)
טַל	**57**	dew, light rain (31)
† (1) כּוֹס	**58**	cup, goblet (31)
*כִּלְיָה	**59**	(always plu.) kidneys (31)
† (1) נָחָשׁ	**60**	serpent (31)
† (1) צַד	**61**	side, flank (31)
שִׂמְלָה	**62**	mantle (31)
לַהַב, (f.) לֶהָבָה	**63**	flame; blade (30)
סִיר	**64**	pot (30)
רִמּוֹן	**65**	pomegranate (30)
בֶּשֶׂם, בֹּשֶׂם	**66**	balsam-tree (29)
זִמָּה	**67**	loose conduct (sexually) (29, 14 in Ex.)
(#)חֲצֹצְרָה	**68**	trumpet, clarion (29, 16 in Chr.)
כְּתֹנֶת, כֻּתֹּנֶת	**69**	tunic, linen garment (29)
*מִין	**70**	kind, species (29, 15 in Gen.)
*עַתּוּד	**71**	(only plu.) male goat, ram (29)
מְעִיל	**72**	sleeveless coat (28)
פֶּחָה	**73**	governor (28)
שִׁטָּה	**74**	acacia (tree or wood) (28, 26 in Ex.)
תֵּבָה	**75**	ark (28, 26 in Gen.) (2)†
אֱוִיל	**76**	fool, stupid person (27, 19 in Prov.)
יוֹבֵל	**77**	ram's horn, ram (27, 20 in Lev.)
יָרֵחַ	**78**	moon (27)
יֶרַח	a.	month (12)
† (1) מָעוֹן	**79**	hiding place, dwelling (27)
סוּף (יַם סוּף)	**80**	rushes, reeds, waterplants (most often in expression: "Reed Sea") (27)
טוּר	**81**	course, row (26)
נֶשֶׁר	**82**	eagle, vulture (26)
נָתִיב, (f.) נְתִיבָה	**83**	path, way (26)
פָּרֹכֶת	**84**	curtain (25, 15 in Ex.)
פִּתְאֹם	**85**	suddenly, surprisingly (25)

III H. Words Occurring 24-10 Times

[1] אִוֶּלֶת	**1**	foolishness (24, 22 in Prov.)
אֵיד	**2**	calamity, disaster (24)
חֹשֶׁן	**3**	breastpiece of high priest (24, 23 in Ex., 1 in Lev. 8 : 8)
יָתֵד	**4**	peg, tent-pin (24)
סַף (2) †(#)	**5**	threshold, sill (24)
עֲבֹת	**6**	rope, cord (24)
*שַׁד	**7**	(female) breast (most often in dual) (24)
אַבִּיר (אָבִיר)	**8**	strong, powerful; stallion (23)
תְּמוֹל (אֶתְמוֹל)	**9**	yesterday (23)
תְּמוֹל שִׁלְשֹׁם	a.	day before yesterday (15)
גַּי, גַּיְא	**10**	valley (23)
הִין	**11**	liquid measure (23, 12 in Num.)
† (1) חוֹל	**12**	sand, mud (23)
כִּיּוֹר	**13**	basin, pot (23)
מַס	**14**	forced service, taskwork, corvée (23)
אוֹי	**15**	woe, alas (22)
[1] (3) אַיִל	**16**	pillar (22, 21 in Ezek. 40-41; 1 in I Kgs. 6 : 31)
אֹפֶל (אֹפֶל), (f.) אֲפֵלָה	**17**	darkness (22)
אֵפֶר	**18**	dust (22)
דָּת	**19**	law, order, decree (22, 20 in Es.)
לְחִי	**20**	jaw, cheek (21)
*מַת	**21**	(only plu.) men (21)
סוֹד	**22**	confidential talk; group of intimates, secret council (21)
*סֶרֶן	**23**	(only plu.) lords (of the Philistines) (21)
אֱלִיל	**24**	gods (idols); nought, vain (20)

[1] Cf. with III G. no. 76 above

[1] For אַיִל (1), see p. 36, III C. 3

בְּרוֹשׁ	25	Phoenician juniper (20)
† (1) חָצִיר	26	green grass (20)
† (2) צִנָּה	27	shield (20)
תֹּהוּ	28	waterless, impassable desert; emptiness (20, 11 in Is.)
† (1) אוּלָם	29	in front of, opposite; but (19)
אוֹן	30	generative power, wealth (19)
מְזוּזָה	31	door-post (19)
עֵנָב	32	grapes (19)
קַיִץ	33	summer; summer fruit (19)
[1] (2) *אַיִן	34	whence? (18)
מֵאַיִן,		
אָנֶה, אָנָה, אָן	a.	whither, where to (26)
אָכֵן	35	surely (18)
בִּירָה	36	citadel, castle (18, 10 in Es.)
חֵךְ	37	palate, gums (18)
כַּד	38	pitcher (18)
מַקֵּל	39	rod, twig, staff (18)
[2] (1) צְבִי	40	decoration, beauty (18)
צַלְמָוֶת	41	darkness (18, 10 in Job)
אוֹב	42	spirit of the dead (17)
אֵימָה	43	fright, horror (17)
בְּרֵכָה	44	pool, pond (17)
גְּדִי	45	kid (17)
גֶּחָל, גַּחַל	46	charcoal, glowing charcoals (17)
(f.), גַּחֶלֶת		
דָּרוֹם	47	south (17, 12 in Ezek.)
חִידָה	48	riddle (17)
חֶרֶשׂ	49	potsherd (17)
צֶלֶם	50	image (17)
קְעָרָה	51	platter (17, 15 in Num.)
† (1) שׁוּשַׁן	52	lily, lotus (17)
תֶּבֶן	53	straw, chaff, fodder (17)
הָלְאָה	54	onwards, further (16)
סַל	55	basket (16)
*פֵּשֶׁת	56	flax, linen (16)
צִיָּה	57	dry country, waterless region (16)

[1] For אַיִן (1), see p. 35, III A. no. 5

[2] For צְבִי (2), see no. 76 below

צֶמֶר	58	wool (16)
שְׂבָכָה	59	net, grating, lattice-work (16)
(#)שַׂלְמָה	60	mantle, wrapper (16)
שְׁאֵר	61	flesh, body (16)
אֲהָהּ	62	(int.) alas! (15)
יֶקֶב	63	wine-press (15)
מֹאזְנַיִם	64	scales, balances (15)
מְחִיר	65	price, hire (15)
† (1) מָן	66	manna (15)
עֲרָפֶל	67	darkness, gloom (15)
רֹמַח	68	lance (15)
† (1) שִׁבֹּלֶת	69	ear of grain (15)
תַּנּוּר	70	stove, fire-pot (15)
תְּרָפִים	71	household gods, idols (15)
אֵיתָן	72	everflowing stream; durable, lasting (14)
(1) כַּפְתּוֹר	73	knob, bulb; capital of pillar (14, 12 in Ex.)
(2) כַּפְתּוֹר		Cf. Crete, 6 t.
לַפִּיד	74	torch (14)
עֹפֶל	75	tumor, boils; knoll, hillock (14)
[1] (2) צְבִי	76	gazelle (14)
קֶמַח	77	flour (14)
† (2) תּוֹר	78	turtle-dove (14, 8 in Lev.)
תַּחַשׁ	79	porpoise; *tachash*-skin (14)
*תַּן	80	(only plu.) jackal (14)
תַּנִּין	81	sea-monster, serpent, dragon (14)
(אַכְזָר) אַכְזָרִי	82	cruel (13)
אֵלָה	83	species of big tree: oak (?) (13)
גַּב	84	back, rim (of wheel) (13)
גְּוִיָּה	85	body, corpse (13)
וָו	86	hook, peg (13, Ex.)
† (1) *חוֹר	87	(only plu.) freedmen, noble ones (13)
חָזֶה	88	breast (13, 8 in Lev.)
טִיט	89	clay, mud (13)
יְשִׁימוֹן	90	wilderness (13)
לֻלָאֹת	91	loops, nooses (13, Ex.)
מַבּוּל	92	heavenly ocean, deluge (13, 12 in Gen., 1 in Ps. 29 : 10)

[1] For צְבִי (1), no. 40 above

Hebrew	No.	Meaning
צְפַרְדֵּעַ	**93**	frogs (13, 11 in Ex.)
שְׁחִין	**94**	boil, inflamed spot (13)
תָּא	**95**	guard chamber (13, 11 in Ezek.)
בֹּהֶן	**96**	thumb, finger, toe (12)
חוֹחַ	**97**	thorns, spiniferous plants (12)
לָבִיא	**98**	lion (12)
קָצִין	**99**	chief, ruler (12)
רֹאשׁ (2) [1]	**100**	poisonous herb, venom (12)
תּוּשִׁיָּה	**101**	effectual working; sound wisdom (?) (12)
† (1) תָּמָר	**102**	date-palm (12)
תִּמֹּרָה	a.	(dim.) palm-figure, ornament (18)
אַיָּל	**103**	stag, buck (11)
בַּהֶרֶת	**104**	spot, blotch on skin (11, Lev.)
גָּזִית	**105**	hewing; ashlar (11)
הֲלֹם	**106**	hither (11)
חָמוֹת (> חָם [1] †)	**107**	mother-in-law (11, 10 in Ruth, 1 in Mic. 7 : 6) (father-in-law)

[1] For רֹאשׁ (1), see p. 35, no. 31

Hebrew	No.	Meaning
סַפִּיר	**108**	lapis-lazuli (11)
*עָמִית	**109**	fellow (of people or company) (11, Lev.)
קָדְקֹד	**110**	vertex, head (11)
שֹׁהַם	**111**	carnelian (11)
*שׁוּל	**112**	(only plu.) skirt, lowest hem of garment (11)
† (1) שָׁמִיר	**113**	thornbush (11, 8 in Is.)
*אֲגַם	**114**	reedy pool, swamp (10)
אִגֶּרֶת	**115**	letter (10)
אֵזוֹב	**116**	hyssop (10)
בַּת (2) [1]	**117**	(liquid) measure (10)
גָּבִיעַ	**118**	cup (10)
חֲלָצַיִם	**119**	loins (10)
עֹרֵב	**120**	raven (10)
פֶּרֶא	**121**	onager (10)
שְׁרִרוּת	**122**	stubbornness (10, 8 in Jer.)

[1] For בַּת (1), see p. 4, no. 4b

Appendix

PROPER AND PLACE NAMES OCCURRING OVER 70 TIMES IN THE OLD TESTAMENT[1]

Arranged in Decreasing Frequency Order

יִשְׂרָאֵל	1.	Israel	אַשּׁוּר	20.	Assyria
דָּוִד	2.	David	שְׁמוּאֵל	21.	Samuel
יְהוּדָה	3.	Judah	מְנַשֶּׁה	22.	Manasseh
יְהוּדִי		Judean	גִּלְעָד	23.	Gilead
מֹשֶׁה	4.	Moses	חִזְקִיָּהוּ	24.	Hezekiah
מִצְרַיִם	5.	Egypt	יְהוֹנָתָן	25.	Jonathan
מִצְרִי		Egyptian	יָרָבְעָם	26.	Jeroboam
יְרוּשָׁלַםִ	6.	Jerusalem	אַבְשָׁלוֹם	27.	Absalom
אַהֲרֹן	7.	Aaron	עֵשָׂו	28.	Esau
פְּלִשְׁתִּי	8.	Philistine	אַחְאָב	29.	Ahab
פַּרְעֹה	9.	Pharaoh	כְּנַעַן	30.	Canaan
בָּבֶל	10.	Babylon	כְּנַעֲנִי		Canaanite
יְהוֹשֻׁעַ	11.	Joshua	יְהוֹשָׁפָט	31.	Jehoshaphat
יַרְדֵּן (#)	12.	Jordan	אֱמֹרִי	32.	Amorite
מוֹאָב	13.	Moab	דָּנִיֵּאל	33.	Daniel
אֶפְרַיִם	14.	Ephraim	כַּשְׂדִּים	34.	Chaldeans
בִּנְיָמִין	15.	Benjamin	אֶלְעָזָר	35.	Eleazar
צִיּוֹן	16.	Zion	אֵלִיָּה, אֵלִיָּהוּ	36.	Elijah
אֲרָם	17.	Aram	בֵּית־אֵל	37.	Bethel
יוֹאָב	18.	Joab	גָּד	38.	Gad
יִרְמְיָה, יִרְמְיָהוּ	19.	Jeremiah	רְאוּבֵן	39.	Reuben

[1] I.e., those not derived from one simple root or stem attested ten or more times elsewhere in the Old Testament (for which see above in the lists).

Addendum: אַבְרָם, אַבְרָהָם , Abram, Abraham, should appear between Nos. 7 and 8 above.

Word Rearrangements

All words in the vocabulary lists marked with (#) should be rearranged as specified below.
(In alphabetical order)

P. 10, No. 34a.	אֶבְיוֹן	Move between Nos. 7 and 8, in list III F., p. 37.
P. 16, No. 10f.	אֲבַל	Move between Nos. 102a. and 103 in list III H., p. 41.
P. 35, III B.1	אֹהֶל	Move between Nos. 8d. and 9, p. 25 (see p. 24).
P. 35, III B.2	בְּהֵמָה	Move between Nos. 5 and 6 in list III D., p. 36.
P. 35, III B.3	גּוֹי	Move between Nos. 14 and 15 in list III A., p. 35.
P. 3, No. 4b.	דְּבִיר	Move to p. 26 as No. 21c.
P. 39, No. 68	חֲצֹצְרָה	Move with its den. to page 28 between Nos. 89b. and 90 (see p. 24).
P. 35, III B.6	חֶרֶב	Move with its den. to p. 25 between Nos. 11c. and 12 (see p. 24).
P. 38, No. 15	טַף	Move with its den. between Nos. 69a and 70, p. 28 (see p. 24).
P. 43, No. 12	יַרְדֵּן	Move to p. 4 as No. 13a.
P. 36, III D, 16	כָּנָף	Move with its den. between Nos. 30a and 31, p. 26 (see p. 24).
P. 36, No. 18, 18a.	כֶּרֶם, כַּרְמֶל	Move between Nos. 14 and 15 in list III E., p. 37.
P. 12, No. 36b.	†(2)נֵבֶל	Move between Nos. 30 and 31 in list III G., p. 38.
P. 28, No. 82, 82a.	נוה	Move between Nos. 68a. and 69 on p. 28.
P. 39, III H.5	סַף	Move with its den. between Nos. 104a. and 105, p. 29 (see p. 24).
P. 37, No. 24	עָפָר	Move with its den. between Nos. 33a. and 34, p. 26 (see p. 24).
P. 40, No. 60	שַׂלְמָה	Move to p. 39 as No. 62a.

Index

All verbal roots are unpointed. Cognates and other words are also unpointed, except in cases of homographs, where sufficient pointing is indicated to distinguish them. The first number (reading from left to right) represents the number of the page on which the word is found; the second number indicates the number of the word on that page. Where two words occasionally have the same number on the same page, their list and section are also given. Addenda on pages 2, 24, 34, and 43 are not included.

א

מ

נ

ס

ע

עצם 16,14
עֶצֶם 16,14a
עצר 13,49
עקב 25,14
עָקֵב 25,14b
עֵקֶב 25,14c
עקר 31,170
עָקָר, עקרה 31,170a
עקשׁ 31,175
עִקֵּשׁ 31,175a
ערב (1) 18,79
ערב (4) 26,34
עֶרֶב 26,34a
עֹרֵב 41,120
ערבה 37, III F. 10
ערה 16,27
ערוה 16,27a
עָרוֹם 16,27b
עָרוּם 31,176a
עריץ 19,102a
ערךְ 9,27
עֵרֶךְ 9,27a
ערל 28,78
עָרֵל 28,78a
ערלה 28,78b
ערם (1) 31,188
ערם (2) 31,176
ערמה 31,188a
ערף 38,46
ערפל 40,67
ערץ 19,102
עשׂב 38,47
עשׂה 4,19
עשׂו 43,28
עשׂור 26,15f
עשׂירי 25,15e
עשׂר 25,15
עֶשֶׂר, עשׂרה 25,15a
עשׂרון 25,15d
עשׂרים 25,15b
עשׁיר 17,36b
עשׁן 29,99
עָשָׁן 29,99a
עשׁק 14,98
עֹשֶׁק, עשׁקה 14,98a
עשׁר 17,36
עֹשֶׁר 17,36a

עת 25,13b
עתה 25,13a
עתוד 39,71
עתר 18,80

פ

פאה 37, III E. 16
פאר 17,29
פגע 13,50
פגר 29,112
פֶּגֶר 29,112a
פגשׁ 20,179
פדה 10,24
פֶּה 36, III B. 14
פֹּה 38, III F. 22
פוח 20,159
פוץ 9,3
פזר 21,228
פח 29,100a
פחד 12,41
פַּחַד 12,41a
פֶּחָה 39,73
פחח 29,100
פילגשׁ, פלגשׁ 38,36
פלא 9,28
פֶּלֶא 9,28a
פלג 31,189
פֶּלֶג 31,189a
פלט 15,146
פליט 15,146b
פליטה 15,146a
פלל 9,29
פלשׁתי 43,8
פן 7,41b
פנה 7,41
פָּנֶה, לפני 7,41a
פִּנָּה 7,41d
פנימה 7,41e
פנימי 7,41c
פסח 28,66
פֶּסַח 28,66a
פִּסֵּחַ 28,66b
פסיל 28,85b
פסל 28,85
פֶּסֶל 28,85a
פעל 10,29
פֹּעַל 10,29a

פעלה 10,29b
פעם 26,35
פַּעַם 26,35a
פצה 20,160
פקד 5,30
פקדה 5,30a
פקודים 5,30b
פקח 18,92
פקיד 5,30c
פר 37,25
פרא 41,121
פרד 15,156
פֶּרֶד 15,156a
פרה 11,16
פָּרָה 37,25a
פרח 14,102
פֶּרַח 14,102a
פרי 11,16a
פרכת 39,84
פרם 18,93
פרסה 18,93a
פרע 19,148
פרעה 43,9
פרק 21,229
פרץ 10,46
פֶּרֶץ 10,46a
פרר 12,38
פרשׂ 9,4
פרשׁ 27,58
פָּרָשׁ 27,58a
פשׁה 18,81
פשׁט 13,67
פשׁע 12,25
פֶּשַׁע 12,25a
פשׁת 40,56
פת 30,157a
פתאם 39,85
פתה 15,147
פתוח 31,177a
פתח (1) 7,42
פתח (2) 31,177
פֶּתַח 7,42a
פתי 15,147a
פתיל 31,178a
פתל 31,178
פתת 30,157

צ

צאן 3,9a
צאצאים 3,9d
צבא 15,3
צָבָא 15,3a
צבי (1) 40,40
צבי (2) 40,76
צד 39,61
צדיק 11,4a
צדק 11,4
צֶדֶק 11,4b
צדקה 11,4c
צהב 26,16
צהר 29,107
צהרים 29,107b
צואר 38, III G. 23
צוד 17,42
צוה 4,20
צום 17,47
צוֹם 17,47a
צוץ 30,148
צוק 21,215
צור 14,118
צוּר 37, III E. 17
צחח 30,160
צחק 16,15
ציד 17,42b
צידה 17,42c
ציה 40,57
ציון 43,16
ציץ, ציצה 30,148a
צל 27,64a
צלח 10,12
צלל (1) 30,161
צלל (3) 27,64
צֶלֶם 40,50
צלמות 40,41
צלע 38,37
צמא 19,125
צָמֵא 19,125a
צָמָא 19,125b
צמד 30,149
צֶמֶד 30,149a
צמח 14,119
צמר 40,58
צמת 20,161

ק

ר

שׂ

שׁ

ת